Crystals & Healing *for the* Serious Seeker

Henriette Maasdijk
FMFSEM, MAST, Cert Ed

Vibrational Healing Foundation

Published by:
The Vibrational Healing Foundation
London W1A 6US

A catalogue record of this book
is available from the British Library.

ISBN 978 0 9547569 5 6

Disclaimer
The information in this book is based upon the author's personal knowledge and experience and is not intended to diagnose, prescribe or treat any ailment, nor is it intended as a substitute for qualified medical advice. If you have a medical problem, or emotional, mental or spiritual health concerns, please consult a qualified physician or a medical healthcare professional. This information is presented at this time with no claim of scientific proof.

All information and techniques are to be used at the sole discretion of the reader. Throughout the book, all exercises have been recommended in good faith. Therefore, in the event that you use the information in this book, the author and publisher assume no responsibility for your actions. This book is for personal use only.

Cover Design by Irinia
Photography © Gareth Thomas

For information about courses:
vibrationalhealingfoundation.co.uk

To all students and practitioners of the subtle healing arts.

Contents

Foreword

I began my training in energy work and inner development over 20 years ago. Back then I was hungry for books about healing that would enrich my knowledge and assist me in raising my vibration. Ultimately, the aim was to understand my purpose and improve my life. Although many good books were available at the time, I never found a book that I felt was complete in its understanding of how healing works and what benefits could be harvested.

Fast forward through the years and now I feel that this book is a reality. The author, Henriette Maasdijk, is a true bastion for the healing arts and esoteric understanding. She has put together this fantastic aid for anyone serious about healing themselves and others. A compilation of over 30 years of teaching experience, this book is the ideal companion for anyone interested in energy work, or who is already training or practising. As a tutor myself, I would also highly recommend it to those who teach others about healing, because rarely will you find such clear and concise explanations on how crystals, colour and sound can be used as healing tools.

I know many healers who have greatly benefited from Henriette's profound teachings over the years, having been instructed and guided in a true healing art. Similarly, those who have received healing from both graduates and students of her school, The Vibrational Healing Foundation, have, without doubt, benefited greatly.

Becoming a crystal and energy healer or subtle energy medicine practitioner is no easy task, and being able to have an in-depth knowledge of the human subtle anatomy e.g. chakras and energy field, both theoretically and practically is essential.

In addition to this, knowing how to sense subtle energies and channel healing, whilst navigating the many non-physical realms, is at the core of any serious energy healing discipline. This book contains all that any serious seeker or practitioner needs to know in understanding subtle energy work and its application. Simultaneously, the wisdom within this book will support anyone on the path towards more light. In short this is an essential work and reference book to anyone who dares to look inward, in the hope of helping themselves and humanity evolve.

Dr Gareth Thomas
Chair
The Federation of Subtle Energy Medicine

Introduction

This book was written to support those who are in the process of training in the fields of crystal and energy healing and related therapies. It is specifically for the serious seeker who finds him or herself on this incredible journey, but it can also be of use as a point of reference for practising healers. If you already have experience in related energy therapies and are not sure if you wish to embark on a lengthy course, this book may also enable you to make a more informed decision.

The subject matter delves into what healing represents, what is involved in healer training, and how to practise safely and responsibly. A large section of the book is devoted to crystals, since using crystals in healing is a more intricate process than many realise. This merits a deeper insight into the subject rather than a 'glossing over' with fleeting explanations. At the end of the book, you will find a comprehensive list of crystals that are most often used by healers, including descriptions of their associated energies.

For those who wish to use crystals for personal interest only, my previous book called Crystals & Healing for Everyone, is for newcomers and contains a number of simple self-healing techniques, a list of crystals, their energies, and a few pages of crystal pictures. I obviously could not avoid some repetition in this new book, especially when describing the crystals; however, you will find both techniques and crystals expanded upon with far greater depth and insight, particularly with a focus on their use for healing.

There are many books about healing, and it is evident that people explain things in different ways, which does not make anyone necessarily right or wrong. This book is based on personal experience, most of which has been confirmed over many years by students, graduates, trusted colleagues, co-workers and clients.

In some of the chapters, information is briefly touched upon before being explained in more depth in subsequent chapters. This is because the teaching of healing and related subjects is best done in stages since most topics consist of various levels. I have also mentioned a few concepts more than once in the book in order to underline their importance and to prevent the reader from having to revert back to previous chapters. The reason the book is in two parts is because energy healing is a complete therapy in itself as is crystal healing.

I have had many teachers, some good and others less so, pleasant and the opposite, genuine or otherwise. All of them have helped me to be who I am now and deserve a big thank you. I perceive every single person I meet, hear about or am aware of as a mirror, guide or messenger and am thankful to all of them, even when the experience is not always easy. I also want to express my deepest gratitude to all those beings and energies that are not clothed in matter, for helping me to carry out my Lightwork and move forward on this path. A very special thank you to the amazing and patient editors, Ann

Hopkins and my daughter Irinia of this book. Their sheer understanding of our work has made it possible for the book to be edited without changing or distorting any of the content.

Finally, I want to thank you, the healer, who is reading this book. I hope you will enjoy both the text and the energy it represents and, above all, that it may inspire you on your healing journey and your path towards ever greater Light.

PART I

THE WORLDS OF ENERGY HEALING

1

About Healing

What is Energy Healing?

Everything in this world can be viewed as energy, which is something that has been established by science for more than a hundred years and validated further by quantum physics. Although this concept implies that we can view ourselves as beings of energy, this has not yet been fully recognized by most people other than in theory. What it means in practical terms is that our physical body is but the densest part of a highly complex system of energy, which is known as our bio-field, electro-magnetic field or in popular terms our energy field or auric field.

The fact that all is energy and that we are far more multifaceted than was recognized until quite recently, and the notion that the whole world can also be perceived as energy and is in essence multi-dimensional, opens up whole new and wondrous concepts of what life on Earth is about. It implies that rather than being 'victims of fate', we can create and co-create our existence to a far greater extent than previously understood. The mystery schools of old were fully aware of these truths, but most of them, until fairly recently, kept this awareness in relative secrecy to avoid clashing with mainstream religious doctrines or other standards that might have led to their persecution. Some also did not wish to share their wisdom because they believed it was only for those who could use it responsibly, and others preferred to keep it for themselves because knowledge brings power. All of the above form the basis of energy healing. None of this is new, and the words written above the temple of Apollo in Delphi say it all 'Man know thyself,' (which nowadays we would phrase, 'Human know thyself'). Such a sentiment indicates that the path towards enlightenment necessitates self-awareness, and this includes self-healing.

When we begin to view ourselves as beings of energy, we become aware that all imbalance in our lives, including the cause of most illness, is held within our energy field, which can be further categorized into a number of specific energy systems. All these energy systems grouped together are referred to as subtle anatomy, which is explored more fully further on in the book.

Every aspect of our life is demonstrated in our subtle anatomy. If we feel well, fulfilled and content, the energies will flow throughout the whole of it without obstruction. Anything amiss, however, including the state of our emotions, thought processes and other concerns will show up in our subtle anatomy and if ignored, can ultimately become the cause of any form of illness.

Although medical treatment may then be required to help the physical anatomy (body) get well, if the cause of the problem is not addressed, symptoms often reappear or the client may stay stuck in an unfortunate life circumstance. This is where energy healing can be of benefit.

Energy healing, as described in these pages, is a treatment that helps activate self-healing and other processes in an individual, which may allow relevant insights and deeper awareness to emerge. It addresses the (energetic) cause of ailments or troubles and the main aim is to support a client with moving through their life experiences with more ease. Healers do not focus on the physical body of their clients, even though it does form part of the energy field and is affected by it. They also do not treat illnesses or other physical symptoms directly.

A well-trained healer is able to evaluate the subtle anatomy of a client and then address issues where indicated. To do this, s/he enters into an expanded state of awareness, links to natural, beneficial energies, links to their client, and then channels the healing energies as appropriate. If the healing is done well, the client's subtle anatomy will be in a much-improved state at the end of a session.

After a session, clients often revert back to habits that were the cause of difficult issues, and so the improvement may not last all that long. Their energy field, however, will retain a memory of the improved state, which can then be reached again with relative ease, once necessary changes have been made. Healers cannot possibly guarantee that issues in their clients' lives will be resolved after a single session, because we all have free will and can continue to think, feel and act with full choice, even if this is not to our benefit. For this reason, healers are unable to state that they can cure or fix anything. Clients do, however, often notice a difference after a session and can make up their own minds if it is worthwhile to come again!

What is Crystal Healing?

Crystal healing is energy healing with the use of crystals, and therefore a highly specialized form of energy healing. The actual procedure is similar, but when crystals are used, the subtle anatomy of a client will experience a highly beneficial and potent pattern of energy during the best part of the session. This is far more intense and, to some extent, longer lasting than can be achieved with energy healing alone. As indicated before, once you have experienced something, you are able to recognize it on subtle levels and then aim towards repeating it. Since our lives consist of innumerable past and present experiences, it is obvious that a practitioner cannot focus on all of these in one session. A crystal healer will proceed with extra care, making sure to work to levels that a client can handle without too much discomfort, because crystals are incredibly powerful and overuse can be counterproductive.

Practitioners may also use a variety of other tools such as colour and sound awareness, flowers or flower essences in combination with crystal and energy healing, depending on their expertise.

Returning to the concept that both crystal and energy healing are essentially about assisting someone in moving through certain life experiences, it makes perfect sense that many healers become interested in serious inner (self) development. When you look within yourself, and work to uncover that which may be holding you back from your own truth and happiness, every part of your life and being can be improved upon. Such inner development includes looking at questions relating to why we exist, where we come from and where we are going once our life on Earth is over. In other words, it is about knowing yourself to the most profound levels possible. Life then becomes a huge adventure, although the path can be quite challenging at times. Memories from other lifetimes may come to the fore, your connection to your Higher Self and also your Soul aspect is enhanced, and the reasons for your present incarnation become more obvious.

An enormous number of books have been written on healing, self-development and other related topics. Although reading these can enrich your life, it is only through personal experience that lasting progress is made. While others can point the way and be of assistance when questions arise, all the work and effort comes from the seeker him or herself. It must also be noted that this path of healing and awareness is open to all and not defined by religions or specific belief systems; everyone has the possibility of integrating their inner development in accordance with their religious or personal beliefs.

To sum this all up in a nutshell, both energy and crystal healers evaluate the subtle anatomy of a client with the aim of bringing this into the best possible balance. This is done with the understanding that the process is to support their clients through life experiences and challenges, rather than 'fix' any issues. We cannot, after all, live someone else's life for them and even if we could, this would negate the reasons for their existence. Our physical body itself is nothing other than the densest part of our entire energy system, and hence it is also ultimately affected by the healing process. To treat it directly, however, requires a completely different skillset, and it is of the essence that boundaries between therapies are respected.

Causes of Imbalance

It goes without saying that a healthy lifestyle, including a wholesome diet, exercise, relaxation and taking good care of one's physical body are imperative for good physical health. This is unfortunately not as straightforward as it used to be, since our world has become quite toxic over the last few hundred years, and we are also increasingly exposed to radiation. More and more people are becoming aware of this, demanding change, and we can only hope this will happen sooner rather than later!

Subtle care is, however, equally (if not more) important, since many (if not most) causes of illness originate on subtle levels. A well-known and recognized example of this is excessive stress. Stress begins with a thought of feeling threatened, accompanied by strong emotions such as worry or anxiety. This is better known as the fight or flight response which releases chemicals such as adrenaline and nor-adrenaline in the physical body. If this process continues over time, it will affect the immune system and physical symptoms can ensue.

It follows that repetitive negative thought processes, accompanied by strong emotions, more often than not result in illness. It also shows that thoughts and emotions have a considerable effect on our physical body and that they can be perceived as energy. The same goes for memories, habits, beliefs and so on, which are all energies that are part of us and our energy field. It is exciting to say the least, when we begin to realise how much influence we have over the state of our health and well-being. How to start using this information is covered a little later in this book, in the chapter about self-healing.

Why be a Healer?

There are a multitude of ways in which people find themselves on the healing path. Many care deeply for the world, nature and humanity, and want to help create positive change. Others have an inborn healing gift, are highly intuitive or sensitive, and have always been acutely aware of the energies that surround them. Some find their way through the hard knocks they have had to overcome, having gained much valuable life experience, determination and compassion. There are also those who are disillusioned with the world around them and in a sense wish to escape, although they usually find their way forward after a while. A number of newcomers perceive the unseen worlds as special or glamorous, until their experiences become more real. Some may have started out in this field as a hobby, and then realise that a whole new world is opening up. There are also those, already mentioned, who are deeply interested in what is termed the mysteries and are curious about why we are here and what life/reality is all about. The list goes on and on, yet it is interesting to note that at the present time, more and more of those who are called to step upon this path are doing so at a much younger age than ever before.

Although I do not advise those younger than their mid-twenties to embark on a profound healing journey, there are always exceptions. There is no cap on advanced age with regard to starting out. Sometimes being older is an advantage because of extra life experience. What is important to acknowledge is that healing is a way of life rather than a nine to five job or a hobby. It is also a path where you never stop learning, because it is a path of actual experience and evolution. There are a few very special and gifted healers, as well as spiritual teachers in the world who were born this way. Most of these are well known, and incarnated for the specific purpose of helping humanity and the Earth itself. There are also a number of exceptional human beings who do their work quietly and anonymously, and I believe that it is largely due to them that our world is still intact.

How to become a Healer

A generation or two ago, not many people knew about healing, and few wanted to train in this field. Those who were interested in the worlds of energy usually joined spiritual groups or similar organisations, and only those over forty years of age were accepted, bar a few extraordinarily gifted individuals. Over the last fifty years or so, this has changed dramatically and there is now a huge amount of information, as well as courses and workshops available about what used to be considered esoteric and often secret knowledge. Although it is a good thing that it is now common knowledge that everything can be perceived as energy, there is a downside to this as well. This is mainly due to the erroneous notion that profound energy work, including energy healing, can be learned via theoretical information, be this on the internet or through reading books. Another such notion is that healer training only takes a short period of time. Although there are excellent short courses that can give one an idea about the worlds of energy and how to use this information in daily life, this is different from following a serious path towards ever greater awareness or seriously developing one's healing gift.

If you are thinking about becoming a healer, it is first of all useful to reflect on what it is you wish to achieve.

Do you wish to add to your general well-being, acquire a new interest, further a natural ability, help others professionally or delve deeply into what used to be called the mysteries? With regard to general well-being, it is indeed worthwhile to read a few books on self-help & healing, and then attend a workshop or short course on the subject you are most interested in. This can also help you determine if you wish to take things further and embark on a lengthy training course. If you want to work professionally in this field, it is advisable to do some research and find out about various courses, as well as meet those who facilitate these. It is important that you feel confident about your course and have a good impression of the main tutor.

To become fully qualified in crystal and energy healing takes a minimum of two years of study and practice, although many healers choose to do this over a much longer period of time. Practical subjects and theories are not difficult to learn, but these represent a fraction of the training, which is currently mostly done over a number of fourteen or so weekends. Intuitive development, assessing the state of human energy systems that cannot be perceived with the naked eye, becoming familiar with many crystalline energies and how to apply these in both simple and complicated techniques, to name just a few topics, does take time. The reason that seven or so weekends are spread over one year, is to give students the chance and personal space to fully integrate what has been covered, and then turn this into actual experience.

The most challenging, but also most fascinating part of healer training, is the often life-changing inner development students experience and the fact that a whole new perception of the world opens up, although this is not always easy to navigate at first. It is therefore important to learn together with other students in a group energy, as well as being able to experience what is discussed in a supervised and safe setting. You will also have the opportunity to make friends, who later on often become trusted colleagues. It is not possible to travel this path alone, and having a few allies with whom to discuss subjects and share experiences that are still considered peculiar by many, is invaluable.

When you are qualified, practising, and content with your life, that is great, and many healers leave it at that. If, however, you wish to take things much further, that is also possible. In the end, even after years of healing and Lightwork, serious seekers know that they have only scratched the surface. The great adventure of healing is never ending, and it is the most exciting, inspiring and wonderful journey one can embark on in full consciousness!

2

The Healer's Energy Field

The first areas to focus on when learning to be a healer are how to maintain one's personal well-being on energetic levels, link to Light energies and channel these safely. This involves being grounded, having a clear and strong energy field and making sure one's space is energetically as clean as possible. We will look at these areas separately.

Grounding

All healers are sensitive as well as intuitive by nature, and often feel more comfortable in dimensions other than the material plane of existence. This is understandable, but as far as healing is concerned, we must make sure we can channel healing energies to the most down-to- earth levels possible, and ensure our clients are brought back to an ordinary state of awareness at the end of a session. We must also be able to explain and take responsibility for our actions, practise discernment regarding subtle energies and not get lost in illusion.

Some other reasons for having one's feet on the ground are to avoid burnout and stay balanced as well as energetically strong. Being more aware of energies than most people is not always easy, and being grounded does help with this. One excellent incentive for healers to ensure they are fully grounded is that the more grounded you are, the 'higher' or deeper you can reach into the worlds of Light and then bring your experiences back into consciousness, so you remember them.

A few indications of being ungrounded are an inability to stop daydreaming for long periods of time; feeling dizzy, nauseous or having heart palpitations when medically all is in order; being oversensitive to light and noise, and not being able to manifest one's plans. Other symptoms are procrastinating; being overly forgetful; falling asleep when meditating and being accident-prone.

There are quite a number of things one can do to help stay grounded. Practising any type of sport, walking, gardening and going to the gym are all very effective. Having a healthy and balanced diet and wearing more earthy colours such as brown, dark green or red are also useful. Herbs such as rosemary and thyme are earthy, and there are many crystals with grounding energies mentioned in the crystal section of this book. Visualization techniques, such as imagining roots growing from one's feet deep into the ground, are something that can be done in a few seconds. A grounding meditation in included in chapter four.

Healers keep their clients grounded by being grounded themselves, and most people feel instinctively much more comfortable in the presence of a grounded person, than in that of one who is not energetically present.

Clearing your Energy Field

Throughout the day we are bombarded with impressions from other people and the environment. In addition to this, we have our personal thoughts and feelings, which are not always of a pleasant nature. Those who work in social care, healthcare or similar professions, often pick up unhelpful emanations from the many different people with whom they come into contact. And those who work in open-plan offices, full of computers and mobile phones that constantly emit unhelpful energies, may be surrounded by work colleagues who have their own difficult issues to cope with. When you travel by public transport, you are closed in with many people, not all of whom are in a good frame of mind or emotion. All such examples indicate that it is necessary for almost everyone to clear their energy field several times during the day.

For healers, this is even more important since those who come to you usually have much debris in their energy field, and you are not served by taking any of this on board. Years ago, I heard of a method of healing, in which the healer would do all they could to take their client's symptoms on board and then heal themselves. As far as I know this is no longer done since many such healers did not always manage to clear themselves fully and became very ill as a consequence. When facilitating healing sessions, always clear yourself before you clients come and again after they have left. It is also advisable to clear and protect your energy field before you go to sleep, since this will not only improve the quality of your sleep, but also that of many of your dreams.

The fastest way of clearing your field is by visualizing (imagining) a waterfall of bright light flowing through the whole of your energy field, washing away anything that is unwanted. After this, it is important to replenish your field, since in energy work one of the golden rules is to never leave an empty space. Some healers use a violet light to clear and then replenish their field with a golden energy. You can do this visualization whilst you are having a shower or at any time you feel it is needed. A more intense clearing method is described in chapter four.

Another cleansing technique is to use breath. Begin by sitting or standing still, and then on the in-breath, breathe up a white light from the back of your feet, until it comes over the top of your head. Then, on the out-breath, let it flow into the earth in front of you, taking with it any debris. You can do this for each of the seven levels of the energy field (more about this in chapter six), moving each breath a little further away from your body. Some healers use the rainbow colours, starting with the red (which in a rainbow is a deep pink), closest to the physical body and finishing with violet for the seventh level.

You can also use sound by way of sounding or playing a Tibetan bowl, clinking a Ting Sha or tapping a chime, and mentally directing the sound to clear your energy field. An excellent note for clearing is the A above middle C, and single chimes of that note are easy to obtain. Another method of clearing your energy field is by lighting a bunch of sage called a smudge stick and wafting this around you. The odour of this is quite strong, but it is very effective for dissipating heavy energetic debris. Some smudge sticks also contain other herbs such as rosemary and lavender, which are just as appropriate. Incense sticks also have a clearing energy, although some of these can leave a stale smell, so you may have to experiment until you find a brand that suits you. There are quite a number of crystals that can help clear your energy field and these are mentioned later on.

I am often asked where the energies that are cleared from yourself, others or the environment go, since energy cannot be destroyed. My understanding of this is that unhelpful energies usually go back into the collective, where they are used as appropriate and energies that pertain to ourselves are often transmuted into a slightly higher note (energetic vibration), especially if we have integrated relevant experiences. The same goes for our clients. If you emit negative energies to another person deliberately or otherwise, these usually come back to haunt you, because what you give out must eventually return to you. The Earth itself is also highly effective in transforming energies in a manner that one could liken to energetic compost. Nothing ever goes to waste, and ultimately the aim for all of us is to reach a higher note. Once this is achieved, the world will change accordingly, which is something many of us are looking forward to.

Clearing your Space

All your possessions as well as the space you live in form part of your energy field. Therefore, ensuring that your home is free from unhelpful energies is essential for your health and well-being. Keeping everything relatively tidy and getting rid of excess clutter is always a good thing, since this helps the energy flow throughout your space. Too much clutter can also stop you from being creative and moving forward, and whenever you want something new in your life, it is vital to make space for this and let go of what is redundant.

As far as energetic debris is concerned, this consists mainly of negative thoughts, emotions and the results of interactions between yourself and others. Such emanations do not just disappear by themselves and must be cleared from time to time. Sound is a very effective method to help dispel such energies. Chimes, Tibetan bells, Ting Sha, gongs, rattles or drums are all excellent tools to use, although you may have to consider your neighbours. While creating the sound, place your focus on the unpleasant energies in the room dissolving or leaving, ensuring that you also address corners since these are areas where energies tend to build up. After you have finished clearing, sound your instrument again, but this time with the intent that positive energies replace those which have been cleared. You will find more on this subject later on in the book.

Smudging with sage and rosemary is also an effective method of clearing undesirable energies in your home. Such smudge sticks are easy to come by, and you can light them and waft the smoke through your home while focussing on clearing. You can also tune a few crystals to help keep your space clear. An Apophyllite cluster is excellent for this since this crystal already naturally emits potent clearing energies. Amethyst absorbs negativity, and Smokey Quartz helps clear heavy-duty energies as well as keep these at bay as much as possible. A large piece of Rose Quartz can be tuned to promote harmony, and Schorl (Black Tourmaline) is the best crystal to help absorb and neutralize static energies from computers and other technical or electrical objects. You tune your crystal by holding it and directing the thought (in this case of clearing negative energies) into it. Crystals that you use to help clear your space must, in turn, be cleansed regularly.

If there is a geopathic stress line running through your house, it is essential to avoid sleeping on top of it or sitting near it for long periods of time. Such negative lines are distorted earth vibrations created by underground streams, sewers or water pipes and can be counterproductive to your health. Information about such lines is not included in this book, but if you are concerned about a possible geopathic line in your home, you could contact the Dulwich Health Society, founded by Rolf Gordon, which is a professional organisation that advises on such issues. One indication that you may have a negative line in your garden or home is that roses will not flourish on it and dogs will avoid lying there. Cats and vermin do not seem to mind such negativity but if in doubt, it is best to check.

If there are others living with you, please add the intent that the energy work you do for your home is for the highest good of all of them, and to the level that they can live with. The reason for this is that not everyone is comfortable with being exposed to high energies in their living space.

Please remember that everything has its own energy, which means that you may from time to time also have to clear your furniture and other objects in your home. You can do this by meditation and channelling Light energies. There is more on this in chapter four. If you have a garden or patio, please do not forget to offer the plants within it healing or Light from time to time, and you may have to clear energies there as well. Where your healing room is concerned, it is a must to clear this after every healing session, not forgetting the couch and all the healing tools you may have used.

Clearing your space at work can be a bit more challenging, and you may have to limit this to your immediate surroundings and your desk. If you cannot place a crystal on your desk, plants are also highly effective at keeping the space around you clear, and you could always put a few small appropriately tuned tumbled stones in the plant pot. Peace Lily is a suitable plant to help keep a room clear of unpleasant emanations and it is easy to maintain.

Strengthening your Energy Field

Although it is important for everyone to have a strong energy field, for healers this is a must. Many sensitive people, therapists and carers often feel drained for no specific reason. Equally, when developing as a healer, many inner changes may occur due to the inevitable expansion of awareness, which can temporarily affect the energy field. It is also essential to maintain a strong energy field and firm boundaries when facilitating healing in order to avoid taking on clients' symptoms or disease patterns. Having a strong energy field helps protect us from unwanted outside influences or, alternatively, protect others from our own unhelpful energies if we are going through a bad patch.

Some of the more obvious signs of having to strengthen one's energy field are: constantly feeling irritated; feeling fearful or overly defensive; feeling drained; losing one's temper too often; having frequent nightmares; feeling threatened for no reason and being easily influenced. Since your possessions also relate to your energy field, being burgled or your car being vandalised, are other signs. People bumping into you or verbally attacking you, even if you have given no offence, are also related to a weaker energy field.

Many healers have a number of different clothes sizes in their cupboard because our bodies, steered by our subconscious mind, are very clever in alerting us to a weakened energy field. Gaining a size, when you have neither changed your diet nor are suffering from an illness, is a sign that you need to strengthen your energy field. Equally, if you are going through a major change in your life, such as changing job or moving house, your energy field will be weak, because the old is dissolving and the new is not yet fully there. Once you have let go of the old, eased away any stresses that such significant changes can bring, and begun to be more comfortable in your new circumstances, your energy field will again return to its original strength.

Intense thoughts and feelings from other people towards you will have a negative impact when you do not have a solid energy field. The way this can manifest is that you may start to feel angry towards someone else for no specific reason. If so, it is usually the person in question who is having angry feelings towards you. All of this is the basis of what is termed ‘psychic attack’, and this subject is covered later in the chapter on negative influences. We are all constantly affected energetically by others as well as by our environment, and this can be in both positive and unhelpful ways.

By strengthening your energy field, you do not create a barrier between yourself and others; instead, you ensure you only take on board that which is helpful and discard the rest. If you need to learn a life lesson concerning a trait that is of a lower vibration (such as a negative emotion), you will not be able to prevent that from entering your space anyway, since it will already reside in you. Take the example of gossip – if you are badly affected by someone else's gossip, it is a good idea to examine whether you gossip about others. If so, you now have the realisation to begin working upon refraining from doing this. Alternatively, you may need to learn to be less affected by what others say about you. It is only a lesson, and once you have dealt with this and integrated it, there will be no further need for you to experience it again.

There are several ways to strengthen your energy field. A popular one is to imagine an oval of Light around you with an outer limit of not much more than one metre (three feet) away from your physical body. This Light must be of a high frequency colour such as electric blue, gold, silver, purple or violet because you wish to keep slower and negative vibrations at bay. Also imagine that the bottom part of the oval is in the ground beneath you and that the inside is as strong as the outside. You can then quietly state an intention that only beneficial energies may enter (and leave) your space. When you are in a crowd or on public transport, you can draw your energy field in even closer, as long as this is to a level that feels comfortable. Whenever you feel vulnerable, you should ensure you are well grounded, as being grounded will also help solidify your energy field. A more profound technique of strengthening your energy field is included in chapter four. There also many crystals, mentioned later on, that can help with this and ward off unwanted energies.

Centring your Energy Field

Another step in maintaining a healthy energy field is to centre it. This is slightly different from strengthening, and healers do this before entering an altered state of awareness, such as linking to higher energies or meditating. You can do this after you have cleared and grounded yourself, by focussing on a point situated slightly behind the sacral area (lower abdomen), while also intending to be in a state of balance. Martial artists do this too as it lowers their centre of gravity, connects them further to the Earth and sustains their balance. When you are centred you feel strong, focussed and fully in charge.

3

The Healer's Link and Guidance

In order to facilitate healing, a healer must be able to link to various energies, channel healing energies, and be able to distinguish between various forms of guidance including the Angelic. These subjects are covered in this chapter.

Linking

Linking to anyone or anything is done via thought. If you think about a person, you are creating a link with that person. The more you focus, the stronger your link. Healing others involves linking to both the Earth and the Light, to your client and to the Angelic or nature.

Linking to the Earth is done by grounding. Linking to Light in this context means linking to the highest energetic vibration. Some call this God; others call it Universal Consciousness, the Source or the Creator. It does not matter what it is called; every person needs to decide upon this in line with his/her personal beliefs. People automatically do this when they pray for someone. The difference between praying and healing is that prayer is asking a 'higher authority' for help for oneself or on behalf of someone else. It does not include the channelling of energies or the use of tools such as crystals. Linking to the Light is done via intent – one thinks and then asks.

One way to start linking to Light is to think of something you find beautiful, such as a flower, a crystal, a sunset or a landscape. This will lift your vibration. You can then link with more ease to the inner worlds. Like everything else, it will take a little time and practice before you are fully comfortable with this, but after a while, you will be able to link in moments. It is, however, essential that you know what it feels like when you are linked. This is called a signature, which will help you notice when there is a need to strengthen your link or even re-link. It will also make you aware when your link is not as pure as it could be. The worlds of energy are vast, and you must create your own personal 'language' and signposts, to know where you are, so you can be safe and secure. One signature almost all healers are aware of during the linking process is a profound stillness, which is much more than just the absence of noise. This stillness can only be described as intense and otherworldly, and is an indication that your link is forming.

I have heard that there are people who are happy for others to link them to particular Light energies, rather than doing it for themselves. I personally would not advise this, since I believe that every single person is unique, has their own specific note, as well as belief system, and needs to lead their life and walk their path accordingly. Someone else's link may not be in accordance with this, which could create complications. Nobody can decide upon the exact vibration of your personal link, nor understand your deepest energetic makeup. What they can do, if able, is give you support and show the way. Regarding healer training, a group leader will show everyone methods for linking, and then this is practised. It ensures that all present can do this for themselves without imposing anything.

There are also some who take drugs in order to reach an altered state of awareness, including linking to other planes of existence. This is a usual procedure practised by Shamans and those in their care, in various cultures around the world. It is not advisable to do this, if you do not belong to such a culture, for the simple reason that your link then risks being distorted. Crystal and energy healers link to different planes and do not need any substances to do so. It is also essential that they stay in control of the linking process and while being linked, unless practising trance. However, this is a rarity in our day and age, and not many are happy to be taken over by other beings.

For a step-by-step method of linking to the Light, you first ground, centre and affirm that only pure or positive energy may enter your space. This is done via thought. If you believe in Angels, you acknowledge them. Then think of what in your belief system is the highest Light and ask to be connected to this energy. Following this, become aware of the stillness and peace that follows, and also note how you feel when you are linked.

There are more exercises on how to link in following chapters.

Channelling Energies

Healing includes the channelling of natural energies. Every single human being can channel energies, but the quality of these energies depends on the overall energetic makeup of the person who is channelling. Someone who is habitually full of anger, hate or similar emotions, cannot channel the same energy frequency as someone who is habitually peaceful, loving or kind. This is one of the reasons healers keep working on their own issues, thereby raising their own vibration as much as possible. It also accounts for the fact that healers usually attract clients who are on a similar or slightly lower vibration than themselves. These clients also often undergo comparable issues. After a period of time, however, a new wave of clients will suddenly appear with a different set of conditions and the healer then recognizes that s/he has moved on a little.

It is often asked where healing and Light energies come from. Some believe they are spiritual or divine energies; others perceive them as the energies of nature, and others deem them to be energies from the Creator. Since we live in a world of energy, this does not really matter, yet it is always prudent for a healer to relate this to their personal belief system.

To channel healing or Light energies, you begin by ensuring your energy field is clear. Then you ground and strengthen it, and follow this with intending that only the best possible energy may enter your space. After this, link to the Light and ask for appropriate healing energies for yourself. Let these energies flow throughout your auric field as well as through the whole of your being, including your physical body. This healing Light will go where you need it most, and can sometimes indicate the area of your energy field to which you may need to pay attention.

If channelling healing for a client, follow the same procedure, but after linking to the Light, also link to the other person and then ask for healing and Light energies for that person. Let the Light flow through the whole of your field, so that in a sense, you become a fountain of healing energies. You can then channel these towards the client as appropriate. It is exciting to sense such energies, and it has happened that healers, the moment they felt the Light flowing from their heart centre, immediately directed it towards their clients. This is not advisable, since by ignoring the rest of your energy field, you risk creating a blockage. Always ensure that you are completely filled with the energies, down to your feet, before you start to channel these outwards.

Some healers believe that they do not need to protect or strengthen their energy field before they channel healing energies, because they are working with positive energies. This is a hazardous misconception, because an unprotected healer risks taking on board disease or other lower energy patterns from clients unless they are fully enlightened. The reason for this is that all of us have occasional negative feelings or thoughts, and like attracts like. If protected, however, these unwanted vibrations will be repelled automatically. We also do not want to channel our personal energies towards clients. In my opinion, only those who are fully enlightened do not need to protect themselves, but they also do not need to channel energies. Being in the presence of such a being would be enough of a healing experience. I have, however, yet to meet anyone who is fully enlightened, so presume, as mentioned elsewhere, that such rare people do their work quietly and unobtrusively.

Guidance

A healer works with various forms of guidance as well as intuition, knowledge and experience. Knowledge, experience and intuition are qualities everyone understands; guidance is another matter. Most people cannot yet clearly perceive or sense energies, which is one of the reasons why confusion can result, especially at the start of healer training.

Guidance may come from many things: a higher intelligence; Angels or other beings of Light; one's Higher Self; one's Soul; members of one's Soul group; animals; nature spirits; relatives or other people who have passed away and, also at times, those who are elsewhere in the world and on a slightly higher vibration than we are. Equally, tapping into 'past lives' or the collective unconscious can be taken for guidance. There are also many energy beings that are not of an entirely trustworthy nature, as well as darker energies that can disguise themselves in subtle ways, and one must, therefore, be careful and discerning.

As mentioned before, sacred knowledge that was usually acquired over many years is now instantly available for everyone, which has resulted in fewer people taking the time and steps to fully experience and integrate such teachings. Grasping the deeper meaning of certain concepts, and learning how to recognize and communicate with outside energies that are not of a physical nature, cannot be achieved instantly. Therefore, it is understandable that newcomers can mistake unhelpful and mischievous beings, residing in what is termed the astral world, for genuine and worthwhile guidance.

Such misdirection is usually done in clever ways, although one of the more obvious ones is to be 'told' that one is special, or given some other form of flattery. When in need of guidance on any matter, it is therefore always necessary to make sure the information received is helpful and can be used in practical ways. There is a notion that once you are linked to the Light and have become aware of a presence, you only need to ask three times if this presence is in accordance with the highest Light. If not, the presence will leave. This method is not completely fool-proof, and has caused many to stumble upon the healing path, either for a little while or in a more damaging fashion. Discernment must always be practised.

Where crystal and energy healers are concerned, it is important to note the following: when assessing a client's energy field, it is our intuition and experience that enables us to perceive what is out of balance. It is, however, the Higher Self (both of the client and our own), that indicates where the point of greatest need is and which parts of the field to address. This is because we, unlike our Higher Selves, cannot possibly perceive everything that is going on in another person, where to start addressing what is out of kilter, and how to avoid tackling too much at once.

Crystals and techniques are always chosen via the knowledge, experience and intuition of the healer, who must be able to fully justify these choices. The quality of the healing ray channelled through the healer is always given by (in my view) the Angelic, which in turn is linked to the highest Light vibration available to both healer and client. Healers have no control over this. How this healing ray is emitted to the client also depends on the actual vibration (state of the energy field) of the healer in question. It is also affected by crystals and other healing tools.

It is important to note that we are not always able to have a clear link, due to fatigue, changes in our lives, difficult emotional or thought processes, ego issues or personal development concerns. The best way to work with any form of guidance, therefore, is to realise that we are fully responsible and accountable for everything we do. The more we grow in awareness, the stronger our link becomes, and it then becomes easier to recognize the difference between various forms of guidance. The best way to work with the concept of guidance is to become aware of different subtle signatures. Such a signature can be a feeling, colour, sound, sudden warmth or coolness or something similar that you experience when you are linked or connected to a guide or the Angelic. Each of these signatures would be slightly different. The more you work with energy, the more you will be able to distinguish between such signatures, and you will be able to recognize what is genuine and what may be questionable.

Not all that long ago, many people in the field of healing and related subjects were considered to have mental health issues, because they spoke about and were aware of energies most people could not perceive. Even a few decades ago, eyebrows were raised when one spoke about healing, and it was wise indeed to keep quiet about the subject of guides or guidance. Fortunately, this has now changed because there is more understanding of the worlds of energy. It is, however, essential for those who are interested in this work to be able to stay down to earth and to practise common sense. It is amazing and inspiring to have access to the higher vibrations, but we live down here and must integrate, as well as use our knowledge and experience for the benefit of our clients, other human beings, the world around us and ourselves.

Angels

Angels have always been an integral part of Humanity in Light as well as shadow. There are many stories about Angels and how they have helped people in difficult circumstances, and many books have been written on this subject. The Angelic realms consist of many levels, each playing their part in the great Universal Plan. Angels are not only strongly connected to us personally; they are also mighty beings in charge of order and beauty in the cosmos. They also oversee nature, the elements, countries and cities, and so forth. Angels have imparted highly important messages, as is well documented in a number of religious texts. Some Angels form part of our world of duality (there being dark Angels as well) and others were human before becoming beings of Light.

There are cultures whose beliefs do not include Angels, but most recognize the energies of and behind nature, so this is just a matter of words. Angels can be regarded as an evolving species, parallel and also interlinked to ours. Unlike human beings, they do not have free will and only act in accordance with what the Light (Universal Consciousness or Creator) dictates. There exists a huge hierarchy within the Angelic kingdom; the highest aspect of this comprises the mighty and fiery Seraphim, known as the Angels of pure love. Although most beliefs assert that there are seven ArchAngels, the four best known are Raphael, Michael, Gabriel and Uriel.

Most healers I know, who have an understanding of the Angelic, usually acknowledge them and ask for help with healing work. This is done quietly and respectfully during the linking process, without making claims about this to clients. There are many stories about Angels coming to help severely ill people who, upon such a visitation, were always fully cured. This is very different from the Angelic 'providing' the appropriate healing ray and being present during a healing session and no healer can possibly take credit for this.

There are many people who, in times of need, call upon the ArchAngels for help, healing or protection. More often than not such help is forthcoming. ArchAngels represent such huge and mighty energies that when they assist humans, this uses only a small aspect of their immense energy. Most people relate the ArchAngel Michael, whose name means 'Who is as God', to protection, and the ArchAngel Raphael, whose name means 'God heals' to healing. Metatron who, before becoming an ArchAngel was a man named Enoch, is regarded as the scribe of God and as being in charge of the Akashic Records.

There obviously exist an equal number of dark Angels out there, and we are certainly inspired by both Light and dark energies, whenever there is an opening for this. We form part of nature by way of our physical bodies and also experience positive, negative and distorted thoughts and feelings, which the Angelic and their opposite personify. I believe that every human being has a Guardian Angel, but also that there are less beneficial energies around, that come into play and influence us whenever we veer away from the straight and narrow! One only needs to look at the world at large to understand this – or similar – concepts. The Angelic also has a specific signature, which is a little different from other types of guidance. Some perceive this energy as gold, others feel it as an energy of bliss or a similar quality. The more you practise, the easier it becomes to not only recognize when the Angelic is present but also to communicate with these beings of Light.

If you want to practise linking to the Angelic in general, first ask your Guardian Angel for help with this. Once you are more aware of your Guardian Angel, it is a good idea to give it a name and work in co-operation with regard to your health and well-being. To link to a higher Angelic choir, ask to be connected to this and trust it. After a while, the energies will become more perceptible.

This is a book about crystal and energy healing, and it is, therefore, not appropriate to elaborate in greater detail on this topic, but suffice to say that if you feel much negativity around you, it is always advisable to ask the Angelic for help!

4

Meditation

Meditation forms an inherent part of energy work because it is all done via our inner world rather than from 'out there'. There are many forms of meditation and we will cover these one by one. Most of them require that you sit in a comfortable chair, for the simple reason that when you meditate lying down, you will probably fall asleep. For all meditation techniques it is essential to ensure you are grounded and that your energy field is both clear and strong. Some people like to hold a crystal or two or light a candle in order to help them enter a state of stillness. Before you start, also ensure you will be undisturbed during your meditation.

Linking Meditations for the Healer

Linking to the Light and/or guidance is always done through meditation and there are a number of ways to do this. Some are brief, others take a little longer. Most healers have their preferred ways and a few of these are mentioned here.

Before you start to meditate, clear your energy field and ground yourself by imagining tree-like roots growing from your feet and the base of your spine deep into the earth. You can also imagine that these roots anchor themselves onto a dark coloured or metallic crystal in the earth. You can make them as thick and let them grow as deep as is comfortable. Having grounded, centre yourself by imagining an oval of energy around you, ensuring that the bottom part of it is also situated in the earth. Your roots may be longer than the outer edge of your energy field which is okay. Always check that your oval is strong and affirm that only positive energy can enter it. Do this initial procedure for all meditations unless otherwise indicated. After this, take a few deep breaths, still your mind and relax. Then reflect on what you believe is the highest Light that exists, and ask to be connected. When you are connected, remember what this feels like, so you have your energetic signature to indicate when you are linked, and how this differs from being in an ordinary state of awareness. After a while this whole process becomes automatic.

Some healers focus on a specific colour that takes them to a high link. You can determine for yourself which colour is the most helpful and then use it in your meditation. Alternatively, you can focus on each of the rainbow colours, starting with red and then orange, yellow, green, blue, indigo, purple, gold and white. Some healers use sound to link and do this by tapping a Tibetan bowl, Ting Sha or tuning fork, and then follow the sound until they cannot hear it any longer, whilst focussing on connecting with the Light. You can also choose a crystal or two to help you link, one to ground your energies and the other to reach the highest note possible. Some healers use a symbol, such as a five- or six-pointed star, to help them link. Please note they are not linking to the symbol itself; it is the significance of it that serves as an aid to connect to far higher Light energies.

A method of linking that takes longer is to focus for a moment on each of the seven kingdoms of nature. Begin with the mineral kingdom and reflect on stones, crystals, glasses, caves, mountains and so forth. After this move to the plant kingdom and include trees, grasses, herbs, plants and flowers. Then focus on the animal kingdom and also appreciate how many different species there are. After this look at our own kingdom, followed by the Devic kingdom (the energies behind nature), then various guides of a high vibration and finish with the concept of 'all that is', which in other words is Light. This is a meditation that you can make as long as you want and by the end of it your link will be strong indeed.

It may be useful to mention the highest aspect of each of these kingdoms. For the mineral kingdom it is the crystals; for the plant kingdom flowers; for the animal kingdom dolphins, bees or butterflies. Some believe it is dogs because they love unconditionally. You can also choose another animal you feel is worthy of this. For our own kingdom, the highest aspect would represent beings such as the Buddha, the Christ, Zoroaster, or people with similar qualities. For the Devic kingdom it is the Angels (who are in charge of it), that represent the highest aspect. For the kingdom of guides and similar beings, you can choose yourself what you believe is the highest representation. The last kingdom is that of pure Light, which includes Love and Truth, but this may also be perceived differently by some healers which is fine.

Another way to link is to focus on each of your chakras, starting with the base and finishing at the crown. Gently breathe a clear light into each chakra (on the in-breath) or, if you prefer, use the traditional chakra colour vibrations. When finished, connect all of them and extend this further into a higher Light. You can do this by imagining the energies from the base of your spine moving upwards (like a column of light) on the in-breath. You may need two or three breaths before you reach the Light.

There are many ways to link and most healers create their own methods.

Reflective Meditation

This is useful when there is something going on in your life and you need to make choices, or if you want to reflect on specific parts of your life. After you have linked, relax and gently focus on what is relevant; and you may get some clarity or deeper insight into certain situations. Have a pen and paper ready so you can take notes. Useful information often comes fast, and if you do not jot it down immediately, you could forget it.

Receptive Meditation

This can be used when you need information about something. After you link, you can ask for guidance on certain issues. Just be still and know that the very first impressions and insights that come are the most helpful. Do not let your conscious thought patterns get in the way and write down what comes to mind. When you do this before you go to sleep, the insight you need may come to mind in the morning or you may have received it in a dream. Please always be discerning and only act on what you feel is right.

Creative Meditation

This is also called visualization. This form of meditation is much used in healer training but also to help clients relax. When doing this for clients, it is important to keep things simple and to remember that the point of the meditation is to relax. An effective way is to lead clients to a safe space of their own imagination, and then at the end of the session bring them back from that space. Always make sure that they are comfortable and, if necessary, give them a choice. Rather than leading them to a beach or a lake and suggesting they go for a swim, give them the choice to sit down and look at the water, or enter it if they feel secure enough to do so. It is advisable to avoid leading clients into caves or over bridges, since this is too profound for a healing session and could turn out to be counterproductive. For yourself you can, of course, always do whatever you are happy with!

Here is one of the very brief creative visualizations most clients like:

Once your clients are comfortable ask them to take a few breaths, breathing in the feeling of peace and on the out-breath letting go of any tension. After this ask them to imagine that they leave the room and step into a sunny meadow filled with flowers. There is a large tree in the centre of the meadow and a space to sit or lie beneath it. Suggest to your clients to sit or lie down and to become aware of the beauty of the landscape. Mention that they are safe, can fully relax and that you will call them back when it is time.

Grounding Meditation

This is a more profound grounding meditation:

Ground, centre and link to the Light and go within. Imagine that you are walking in a forest. The trees are very high and although it is daytime, the light is slightly muted. You enter a small clearing where there are several oak trees. The ground is moss-covered and you sit down beneath one of the trees, lean against it and ask it to help you to ground yourself. Roots are now forming from the base of your spine and the soles of your feet and these are as long as the tree is high and are intertwining themselves with its roots. On each in-breath, you receive strength from the tree, and your out-breath in turn nourishes it. Put your hands on the moss and feel how connected you are with the Earth. There is a small stone next to you on the ground and you pick it up. You feel the solidness of this stone, which helps you to ground even more. Once you feel fully grounded, thank your tree and nature and walk out of the forest, back into your room and re-ground.

Clearing Meditation

If you feel the waterfall meditation is not effective, this is an alternative:

Ground, centre and link to the Light and enter your inner landscape. See yourself standing in a big meadow. You can feel your feet on the grass and know that there is a thick layer of earth underneath the grass. Ask the earth to absorb the debris and redundant patterns that are in your energy field and become aware of this happening. It then starts to rain and the drops flow through the whole of your energy field, taking away any debris that is still there. The rain now stops and you become aware of quite a strong breeze, which blows away any other residue of negativity or unhelpful issues in your energy field. This then stops and you find yourself standing in a violet coloured fire, which burns away anything else that you can let go of. This is not painful, because it is a spiritual fire. When finished, you find yourself standing quietly in the meadow and now ask your Guardian Angel and the Light for the appropriate energies to replenish your energy field. Let this healing Light flow right through and around you, including your physical body. After this, thank the Light, the Angelic and the elements, come back into an ordinary state of awareness and ground yourself.

Protection Meditation

This is a more thorough meditation to strengthen your energy field and is appropriate when you feel you cannot keep lower vibrations at bay:

Ground, centre and link to the Light and go within. Focus on the first layer of your energy field and imagine this as a brilliant white light and cover the outer edge with a mirror in the way that should someone look at you, they would see their own reflection in this mirror. Then, a little further from the mirrored edge, fill the space with beautiful rainbow colours and also cover this second layer with a mirror. Fill the third layer with a shiny golden light and the fourth layer with a sparkly light pink or light green colour and cover each of these with a mirror. Fill the fifth layer with a blue colour and this time cover the edge with silver. Fill the sixth layer with a deep purple and cover the edge with a shiny gold. The last layer is filled with a very pale gold. You cover this with the most brilliant white Light you can imagine and firmly state you are now fully protected. Make sure the bottom part of your now very large energy field is anchored deep in the ground beneath you, and then draw it in, towards your physical body, as is comfortable. After this, come back into an ordinary state of awareness and ground yourself.

You can change the colours as you prefer, as long as you make sure they are of a high vibration.

Observing the Self Meditation

This is useful for healers to ensure their energy field is as much in balance as possible. After you have linked, focus on each part of your subtle anatomy and perceive the state of it. If anything feels uncomfortable you can then breathe Light into that part. You can include your physical body in this meditation. If you find there is a fair amount that is not as it should be, use one of the self-healing methods that are described further on.

Relaxation (Stress Release) Meditation

Most of us have periods where we are suffering from excessive stress. Therefore, a relaxing meditation is useful to incorporate in your self-help techniques. You could focus on certain body parts, starting with your feet: tense these and then relax them. Always finish with your head and include your jaw muscles. Alternatively, you can take yourself to a landscape, lie down beneath an oak tree, or any other favourite tree, and ask for an appropriate and relaxing Light energy to flow through and around you. Whilst this is happening, focus on each body part in turn and also play relaxing music. It is always worthwhile to create your own relaxing meditations and listen to these when you are resting, especially if it is okay to fall asleep!

Stillness Meditation

This is what the ultimate experience of meditation is supposed to be! After linking put yourself in a state of 'being'. No thoughts, feelings, imaginings, visuals etc. Just be. This is not easy and it may take time and practice to get there. Once you have mastered this form of meditation it may well become your preferred one!

Walking Meditation

You can do this in nature, but if you are not experienced, it is advisable not to link to Light and to stay in full conscious awareness. Ensure you are well grounded, centred and protected and then walk, only focussing on the present. Some healers do this whilst they are connecting to various energies of nature, communicating with these or exchanging healing energies. For newcomers it is sensible to sit down on a bench whilst doing this!

Strengthening your Inner World Meditation

You do this by focussing on your five senses in your inner world. You can imagine you are in your inner landscape and then try to get a detailed view of all that is in there. If you have not yet thought of an inner landscape, just imagine a beautiful place in nature in which you are happy to spend a little time. Then become aware of the sounds in your landscape, such as birds chirping away, the humming of bees or the sound of a waterfall. Also notice the various scents of the flowers, the grass, hay or anything else. Pick an apple from a tree and eat it, focussing on the taste or find some other fruit if you do not like apples. Where the sense of touch is concerned, feel the wind blowing through your hair, or the texture of grass or sand beneath your feet. Just make up your own version.

It can also be helpful to find out which inner sense is most difficult for you and concentrate on that a little more. The inner senses of touch, hearing and sight are the most important, although there are people who often get a sense of taste or smell in their meditations or healing work that conveys meaning to them.

Open Eyes Meditation

Meditating with your eyes open can take a while to master. It is a must for healers to practise, since they have to monitor what is going on, and notice when a client is uncomfortable during a session. Another reason to practise this form of meditation is that it can assist you in bringing the two (inner and outer) worlds together. At times we react to challenges in ways that we may have good reason to question later on. If we then enter a reflective meditation, we are usually shown a different, and more worthwhile response. When you are aware of your inner world, whilst living your ordinary life, and can link in the blink of an eye when necessary, you are in a better position to avoid making mistakes when challenged. This form of meditation is also helpful when you want to practise your walking meditation to a more profound extent.

5

Being Intuitive

Every single person on the planet has intuitive abilities, although many have repressed these since childhood in our modern-day society. Intuition is our sixth sense and a quality that is essential with regard to being aware of and working in the field of subtle energies. The way to strengthen this sense is through practice and meditation. Other words for intuition are 'psychic' and 'sensitive' (to energies).

Most people who express an interest in energy healing, are by nature already more sensitive than most, but it may take a little extra effort to gain the experience necessary to navigate the worlds of energy without becoming confused or ungrounded. Being highly sensitive does have a downside, since you are so much more aware of what is going on around you. This includes the strong feelings and thoughts that emanate from others, and also those that form part of the collective. It is not so much the actual feelings and specific thoughts that one becomes aware of, but the energetic quality of these. If not of a positive nature, these energies tend to come across as unpleasant or even threatening. Students who are starting out, usually confuse such energies with their own feelings and thoughts or, alternatively, believe that they are under some form of attack. Places that have strong unpleasant energies or difficult issues that are occurring in the collective can also have quite an impact on an intuitive person, and it takes time to recognize and deal with such perceptions.

Many healers initially get caught up in what is termed the glamour of subtle energies. Feeling more 'special' than others or losing a healthy discernment are the most common examples. There are also those who mistakenly believe they are receiving messages or channelling information from historical figures, ArchAngels or well-known religious leaders. Those who have gained more experience know what to look out for, and how to discern between what is genuine and what is questionable with a little more ease. It is all a learning process, and the best way to avoid most pitfalls is to make sure that you are grounded and your energy field is strong. Another good practice is not to take anything at face value. Intuitive development is about becoming familiar with the worlds of subtle energies and learning to use this ability safely and responsibly.

It is essential to verify that what you glean from the worlds of energy is helpful, and also that it can be used effectively. If any form of guidance indicates something that you do not understand, or are not comfortable with, ask for an explanation, and if this is not forthcoming, let it go. Equally, all you learn from your tutors can only be integrated in accordance with your own values and what you resonate with. Intuitive development is not about religion or beliefs and you are the one who decides what to accept and what to leave aside. Although there is much valuable information out there regarding development, crystals, healing and other subjects, there is also much information which can lead you up the garden path, and being circumspect is definitely a must. Never hesitate to ask questions, and if reasonable answers are not forthcoming, move on.

When you start to train as a healer, it can happen that you become a little over-sensitive for a while. When this occurs, it is best to stop all energy work and focus uniquely on the material world for a few days, or however long it takes to feel down-to-earth again. Some of the signs of over-sensitivity (with regard to healer training) are: experiencing thoughts and feelings that are not your own, including those of the collective; mild anxiety for no reason; light-headedness; oversensitivity to noise and Light (even when you think you are well grounded); answering people's thoughts rather than their questions in communication; living too much in the worlds of energy and taking everything too seriously. Another quality to develop, if you do not have this already in abundance, is a sense of humour. When things become a little too intense, you can use this as an outlet. Laughter is also very effective against most forms of negativity.

If you are highly psychic, and can perceive as well as communicate with those who have departed this world, you could decide to train as a medium. Mediumship is different from healing. It is a natural talent that can provide enormous benefit to those who are grieving, or who have unfinished issues with deceased relatives or friends. Unfortunately, practising mediums must nowadays include in their advertising a statement that they form part of the entertainment industry. The reason for this is that they cannot always provide proof that what they advertise is true. I find this sad, because genuine mediums have a lot to offer. Training involves developing one's gifts of clairvoyance (inner seeing), clairaudience (inner hearing) and clairsentience (inner sensing) to a great degree, as well as learning to control these. Sitting in a circle for a number of years with an experienced and trusted teacher is the usual way to do this. Mediums most often link to what is termed the astral world, which is the closest (energy) plane of existence to ours. Healers mainly link to other levels, which is why it is important to be aware of these differences which will be explored in chapter nineteen.

There is also a form of mediumship that is done in trance, and which is mostly about giving people guidance about their life. If you have a talent for this, it is essential that you have a highly experienced and respected teacher. You must have a strong energy field in order to be able to do this safely, and be utterly secure about the guide who will speak through you. If you are fragile in any way, or attracted to what is termed 'glamour', please refrain from doing this type of work. The reason for this is that, although with your agreement, you are taken over by such a guide. As mentioned already, there are devious energies out there which can disguise themselves as benevolent in subtle ways. An auric or clairvoyant reading can be just as effective, without the need for being 'invaded'.

There are a few individuals who practise trance healing and I know of only one person in England, who is a well-known psychic surgeon and highly respected. This form of healing is not allowed in most healing organisations in the UK, since it goes against their code of conduct for good reason. During an ordinary healing session, guidance or the Angelic never take over or 'possess' a healer they only assist in the process.

Finally, you may be practising psychometry, giving psychic readings or using Tarot cards, providing clients with certain insights to what is going on in their life. If this is the case, please note that when you are in the process of healer training, your ability may lessen for a while because you will be using your energy system in a different manner. Once you are well into your training and comfortable with this new way of working, your reading abilities will return with a vengeance!

With regard to these various intuitive abilities and practices, it is also essential to put the necessary boundaries in place when you offer more than one of these. If you are both a medium and a healer, you must not combine these skills in one session. If your client wants both healing and a reading, s/he will have to book two separate sessions. If you are qualified as both a counsellor and a healer, you must only practise one of these during a session, since they are different therapies that require different skills. The same goes for any other similar therapies.

6

Subtle Anatomy

The study of regular anatomy and physiology is about the structure of the human body and the function of its various parts. It is moderately straightforward compared to the study of subtle anatomy, since everyone's physical body parts and their function are similar. Most energy healers study a simple book about this subject, in order to learn the terms for physical body parts and some of the dysfunctions, so they do not have to unnecessarily ask their clients for clarification when they mention issues. They must, however, have an in-depth knowledge, understanding and experience with regard to subtle anatomy and subtle physiology.

Subtle anatomy and subtle physiology are about the structure of the human energy field and the function of the various systems within this field. This field, which exists around every human being, is also called the bio-field, auric field, aura, electromagnetic field or subtle energy field. The terms energy field or auric field are used throughout this book in order to avoid confusion. It is true that everything that occurs in our subtle anatomy will eventually have an effect on our physical body, and that all our life experiences in this world of matter affect our subtle anatomy, but the two subjects are separate. Most medical doctors do not know anything about subtle anatomy because they do not need this for their work and are probably not even aware it exists.

Subtle anatomy is far more complex than ordinary anatomy, since only a tiny part of it can be perceived by the naked eye, and the whole of it is in constant motion. Equally, the function of every part in the auric field relates to life experiences rather than physical functions. Although one can generalise with regard to where every part of the field is situated, each individual's experiences are unique, and can therefore not be compared to anyone else's. The whole field incessantly demonstrates what is going on in our life on emotional, mental, subconscious and spiritual levels. This includes habits, memories, beliefs, ancestral issues and all our experiences both past and present.

Those who practise healing are able to perceive this field, assess the condition of it, know how to address any imbalance and are aware of how the various parts interrelate. If they use tools such as crystals, they also know how to apply these powerful energies correctly and to the level that their clients are comfortable with.

The human energy field consists of a number of layers called subtle bodies, energy centres called chakras and energy pathways called gridlines. We will look at each of these systems separately. There is also a well-known and highly complex energy system called the meridians.

Meridians

Meridians are energy pathways along which energy points are situated, that interpenetrate the physical body and directly relate to physical organs. They form the basis of acupuncture, which is a therapy that has been practised in Eastern Medicine for thousands of years. Acupuncture is an alternative form of medicine, which means that those who practise it diagnose as well as treat physical symptoms. There are also a few forms of energy healing therapies that address the meridians directly. Energy tapping is one of these. The energy systems that are covered in these pages, however, are of a more subtle nature and, although they also eventually relate to the physical body, they do so in a less immediate and direct manner. Since crystal and energy healers do not diagnose or address the physical body and physical symptoms directly, the meridian system is not included in these pages.

The Auric Field as a Whole

The auric field as a whole represents the overall energetic makeup of a person. This can be strong, fragile, overbearing, refined, full of debris, damaged or in any similar state of being. It is the first impression a healer gleans from their client and very important, since it often indicates which tools or techniques can be safely used or what must be avoided. This field extends around three or four feet (a little more than a metre) around a person if s/he is in an ordinary state of awareness. When focussing on spiritual issues, giving or receiving healing or doing other types of energy work, it will extend much further. One can perceive the field as a large egg made up of energy, the bottom part of which is (or should be) situated in the ground.

An ideal auric field is strong, vibrant, energetic and exudes radiance. An example of this in daily life is when you meet someone new, and feel an immediate liking for him or her. Alternatively, you can have a few initial doubts about such a person. When you then spend a little time together, this initial impression often changes, because you then focus on what is communicated vocally. Since most of us mask our true thoughts and feelings, you may find you actually like what this person has to say, and feel that your initial doubts were off the mark. Much later, however, something may happen that confirms that your initial perception was spot on! With regard to healing, this first impression of the overall subtle energies of an individual can come across as strong, fragile, damaged, stressed, grubby, weak, unprotected or any other such qualities. This, more often than not, gives you an initial idea how to proceed with the session.

Subtle Bodies

If you look deeper at the auric field, it can be divided into seven layers. Each of these relate to what is or has been going on in our life on every single level. The layers are superimposed, each one being of a finer or more subtle nature than the preceding one.

The Etheric Body

This layer is situated closest to the physical body and interpenetrates it. If you observe a person sitting or standing in front of a white or dark background, you can see it with the naked eye. It looks like a misty glow around the body, extending a few inches outward. This layer introduces energy into the physical body and also demonstrates its health and vitality. If anything is out of order, grey or black shadows can be perceived within it. Healers sometimes address this layer in order to clear debris or blockages, infuse it with energy or help trigger the body's natural healing processes where there are minor issues.

The Emotional Body

The next layer, also called the astral body, is more fluid than the etheric body. It is the seat of our emotions and feelings, and demonstrates these, when all is well, by way of beautiful, vibrant rainbow colours. Some individuals can perceive this layer with the naked eye and, although superimposed upon the first layer, it extends around three to four feet outwards from the physical body. It also relates to our dreams and, to a certain extent, creativity. Strong, negative emotions can be perceived as murky and distasteful colours in this layer. It is interesting to note that our emotions express themselves in colour, which may be one of the reasons why we often feel the need to wear different colours.

The Mental Body

This is the seat of both conscious and subconscious thought and the last part of the field that can be perceived, by those who are sensitive, with the naked eye. The colour varies from a bright yellow to a golden hue, but only if all is well. If not, dark streaks or a dirty mustard colour can cloud this part of the energy field. It is rare that this body is clear of obstruction, and some argue that it should be subdivided into two parts. All our mental input, constant thought processes and patterns demonstrate only one part of this layer. The subconscious mind, which contains memories, habits and most of our experiences, and can therefore be regarded as our 'database', forms the second part of this third layer, and this is where energies become often stuck.

The mental and emotional bodies are closely intertwined and not always easy to distinguish from each other. The cause of much, if not most, imbalance and unhelpful patterns in our daily life relates to these two layers. It is important to recognize that these layers, which represent our emotions and thoughts, have a strong and sometimes immediate effect on our physical body. The next four layers are of a much finer substance but no less important.

The Higher Mental Body

This is the seat of inspiration, compassion, higher ideals, unconditional love and the perception (in an experiential fashion) that ultimately all is one. The colours can be perceived with the inner eye only and are of a softer and finer vibration than those of the emotional body. This layer also relates strongly to the arts and to anything that requires inspiration. It is interesting to note that this layer is also the one where Angelic influence, and what is termed guidance, can make itself known with more ease. Where part of the lower mental body can be considered as structure, this higher level is more about beauty. When you look at a beautiful sunset and you feel uplifted, you are experiencing and emitting energies that form part of your higher mental body.

The Causal Body

This layer is the seat of our blueprint and can, when appropriate, show us the purpose of our incarnation. Early childhood experiences are stored here, as are what is termed 'past life' or 'other life' experiences. It is also the layer from which one can start to access the 'Akashic Records', also known as the 'Hall of Records'. This is a vast inner space where all our experiences during this and all other lives are stored. This fifth layer interpenetrates all the other layers as well as the physical body. The colour of the causal body, which can only be perceived with the inner eye, is a cobalt blue with hints of silver. This layer relates strongly to major life changes and deep-seated or long-term issues that can be difficult to shift.

The Spiritual Body

This body relates to our religious beliefs, spiritual wisdom and knowledge. It is where we strongly perceive the influence of the Angelic and other beings of Light. It is also the seat of idealism, higher intuition, vision, channelling of 'spiritual' information and prophecy. The colours are even more luminous than those of the higher mental body and mainly consist of soft Mother of Pearl, although that is a pale reflection of what the colours are actually like. It is somewhat difficult to distinguish from the seventh layer, because these parts of the energy field vibrate at very high levels and are therefore not all that easy to access.

The Divine Body

This seventh layer holds the whole of the auric field together and is therefore the most important one. It is not just the strongest layer, but also the most refined, and can be perceived with the inner eye as a luminous pale gold. It represents our highest aspect and therefore relates to the essence of our Soul and also to what some perceive as the Higher Self. It feeds and protects the whole energy field and is ultimately the layer that gives life to all the systems, including the physical body. It also strongly relates to the crown chakra and is therefore the link to all that is or a 'Higher Light'. Religion does not come into this because this layer relates to what any individual believes or intuits to be the highest form of Light, Consciousness and Love.

There exists one other layer, consisting of two parts, but this is not always apparent in each individual and will be looked at further on.

It is valuable for anyone to have an idea of what these layers represent, but for serious seekers or healers, it is essential because they must be able to gauge the state of the various layers within themselves (and their clients) and understand the significance of anything that is out of balance. This is such an important subject that it will be covered later on in chapter nine.

Chakras

Chakras can be likened to vortexes of spiralling energy. There are seven major ones that are situated along the spine. Six of these are connected via three subtle energy pathways, named Ida, Pingala and Sushumna, which are intertwined along the spine, starting at the base and ending at the top in the medulla oblongata. These pathways are associated with the goddess Kundalini. Sushumna is the central pathway, Ida represents the feminine principle, also named yin, and moves upwards from the left side of the central channel. Pingala represents the masculine principle, also named yang, and moves upwards from the right side of it. Some say this varies for men and women, but that does not make a difference with regard to crystal and energy healing. Both channels weave their way upwards, forming and connecting the first six chakras. A Western representation of this is the caduceus, which is a staff with two snakes winding themselves upwards around it. At the top of the staff there are two wings that represent the seventh chakra, which is situated above the crown of the head. The three channels also epitomise the three primary colours, blue, red and yellow, for the centre channel, yin channel and yang channel respectively.

The chakras relate to us in terms of how we take on board everything that happens in our life, process and integrate this, and then express or manifest it in the (our) world. Chakras can be perceived as spirals or cones of energy that spin in both clock-wise and anti-clockwise directions; one direction relates to how we respond to new experiences, and the other to how we express these (once integrated) in our life and the world. The spin of the chakras is more multidirectional, but in our 3-dimensional world this is not as yet apparent. Each chakra spins faster than the preceding one, the slowest being the base chakra. There are various levels within each of these energy centres, which relate to where we are with regard to our many life experiences, past, present and new. In addition to this, there are three main points of access, also called gateways that clearly show where a specific issue within a chakra that needs to be addressed is situated.

It is rare that the whole system is in optimum balance, for the simple reason that there is always something going on in our life. The well-known term 'balancing chakras', is therefore not a fully accurate description, because nobody can balance (or live) our life experiences for us. What experienced healers can do, however, is support us though certain life experiences and challenges, by addressing imbalances in related energy centres and/or elsewhere in the energy field, to levels that a client is comfortable with.

Chakras can be blocked to various degrees, spinning too slow or too fast to various degrees. They can be too open, traumatised, in acute change or, in severe cases, badly damaged. Chakras contain all rainbow colours, although each one demonstrates one overriding colour vibration. Chakras are also (loosely) related to certain body parts and physical symptoms, but this notion is not used by healers when they assess what is occurring in this energy system. The body parts are mostly close to the chakra in question but, if for instance, someone has a problem with their knees (which are nearest to the base chakra) it is more likely that there is an issue in the throat centre rather than the base. Equally, if someone suffers from headaches, which some say relate to the crown or brow centre, more often than not it is the base or solar plexus chakra that needs work. Actual sight relates to the solar plexus rather than the brow chakra, which is another example. It is for this reason that few body parts and symptoms are mentioned in these pages with relation to the energy systems, and only those that are not obvious.

Below is a list of the chakras, their main functions, a few positive and negative qualities and a few other relevant remarks.

Base or Root Chakra

This energy centre is situated at the base of the spine and can be perceived as a cone of energy spiralling towards the ground. Its overriding colour vibration is a vibrant red and it relates to issues of survival, belonging to a group, being grounded and able to turn one's plans into reality. It is also associated with issues of security, self-preservation and stability. Some of the negative qualities are self-centredness, greed, violence and feeling insecure with regard to one's place in society. It relates to the element of earth and the sense of smell and is associated with the actual Earth itself.

Sacral Chakra

This energy centre is situated roughly two inches below the navel and, like the next four chakras, can be perceived as a cone of energy spiralling outwards from both the front and the back of the body. Its overriding colour is a vibrant orange and it relates to creativity, pleasure, sexuality, desire and money. It is also connected to how we relate to others and the assimilation of ideas. Some of the negative qualities are over-indulgence, jealousy, envy, a lack of purpose, sexual and money issues. The skin is linked to this chakra and it relates to the element of water and the sense of taste. It is also associated with the Moon.

Solar Plexus Chakra

This chakra is situated a couple of inches above the navel and relates to personal power, self-esteem and our ego. It is also linked to authority, self-control, laughter, warmth and radiance. Some of the negative qualities are fear, anger, a lack of confidence, being judgemental, perfectionism, controlling behaviour and being overly intellectual. This centre relates to the element of fire and the sense of sight and its predominant colour vibration is yellow. In those who have reached a degree of profound inner wisdom, this is more of a golden hue. The solar plexus is also associated with the Sun.

On a deeper level, this chakra relates to the subconscious mind, which is the place where all our experiences and memories are stored. This may be one of the reasons why it is so rare to find someone with a solar plexus that is fully in balance with the rest of the system. It is also interesting that a very hard knock in the centre of the solar plexus can kill someone who is physically fragile.

Virtually every one of us has ongoing issues in one or more of these lower centres. They relate most to what is going on in our everyday life. If every human being had a balanced approach to issues of survival, money, sexuality, relationships, control and power, the world would definitely be a better place for many, and we could then focus more on the deeper aspects of life! The three lower chakras also (loosely) relate to the first three levels of the auric field and the next four to the higher levels.

Heart Chakra

This chakra is situated in the centre of the chest (between the nipples) and relates to unconditional love, nurturing, compassion, forgiveness, balance and harmony. It is also associated with group consciousness, contentment, peace, openness and clairsentience. Some of the more difficult traits are repression of love, grief, hatred and similar qualities. This centre relates to the element of air and the sense of touch. Its main colour vibration is a vibrant green but this can be pink in some individuals and gold in those who have reached a profound level of awareness. This chakra also serves as a bridge between the three lower and three higher ones. The saying 'coming from the heart' relates to this chakra, although on the most profound levels this means being fully aware (at all times) that we are all one, and acting accordingly.

Throat Chakra

This chakra is situated in the hollow of the throat and the cone of energy spiralling at the back is slightly higher than the spiral at the front. It relates to communication, change, higher will and creativity and is also associated with creative expression in speech, writing and other arts, honesty, reliability and loyalty. Some of the more negative qualities are communication problems, ignorance, knowledge used unwisely and a lack of discernment. It relates to the element of ether and to the sense of hearing, including clairaudience. The overriding colour is a sky blue tinged with silver. Often, when we are in a state of change, we may get a cold or a scratchy throat which can indicate the need to release something and to welcome the subsequent change rather than resist it.

Brow Chakra

This centre is situated between the eyebrows (where they would meet), and relates to intuiting, perceiving energies with the inner eye and clairvoyance. Other qualities are imagination, insight, wisdom and concentration. Some of the negative traits are lack of concentration, cynicism, certain fears and being overly detached from the world. The overriding colour vibration of this centre is a midnight blue and it relates to Light and intuition (sixth sense). It is also linked to the left eye and the lower brain. Since healing involves perceiving energies with the inner eye, this centre is often out of kilter during stages of intuitive development.

Crown Chakra

This centre is situated slightly above the head and relates to unification with the higher self, one's link with the Light and various forms of guidance. Other qualities are Divine wisdom, selfless service, perception beyond space and time and continuity of consciousness. The negative aspects are confusion, depression, hesitation to serve and being misguided. It can also relate to psychotic behaviour, insanity and certain forms of migraine. The overriding colour is a deep purple, although many also perceive this centre as gold. The halo depicted around the heads of saints is an expression of this chakra. It relates to cosmic energy and to 'instant knowing' and is linked to the right eye and upper brain.

These seven main chakras are highly complex and each consists of various levels that relate to an individual's ongoing life experiences. They are all interrelated and in constant movement. Where the colour vibrations in the chakras are concerned, the overriding colour described is the one with regard to the lower levels of each chakra. On higher levels these colours become more luminous, as do the other colours that are contained in each of them.

Gridlines

This energy system relates to how we move through our experiences, and it also links us to everyone and everything in the world. If you look at an atlas, you will see a grid of vertical and horizontal lines superimposed on the pictures of the continents. This is an excellent analogy for how the grid system can be perceived, including on personal levels.

The vertical line I represents the male principle and the horizontal ones —— the feminine principle. If you join these lines together you get a cube, which in sacred geometry represents the Earth. This therefore also represents the world of duality. The concept of dualism in ancient Chinese philosophy (Wikipedia) is represented by the well-known yin and yang symbol. This is a circle, divided by a curved line. One side of the circle is black, representing the feminine principle, yin, and the other side is white, representing the masculine principle, yang. There is also a small white circle in the black area and a small black circle in the white area. These indicate that yin and yang also contain their opposites.

If one translates this into what is and has been going on in the world, one can say that the horizontal lines are a representation of a matriarchal society and the vertical ones of a patriarchal society. Neither express the balance we need in order to evolve. This is not just about men or women it is about what these energies represent, and they ultimately must complement one another before we can evolve towards a higher note. This slightly faster or higher vibration can be viewed as two slanted lines, X that one can superimpose on the squares of the grid. A suitable word for these two lines is androgynous, which means partly male and partly female and, in a sense, transcends the concept of duality.

With regard to human beings, this superimposed X could relate (amongst other things) to equality between male and female principles; and there are already many people who have developed a balance between their male (yang) and female (yin) sides. In Western psychological terms the male energy is called our animus and the female energy our anima. In our current society we can see this in the successful business woman and the husband or partner who is not averse to helping with childcare and around the house to name just two examples. Even a few decades ago this would have been quite rare.

If two people (regardless of their gender), who are fully balanced in this manner, form a partnership, this is incredibly solid, because it represents an equal partnership. There is then no need for any power games or manipulative behaviour, since both parties are and feel as strong, confident and capable as each other. To date this has started to emerge mostly in the Western world and hopefully will continue across the Globe. In the West, this concept is symbolized by the equal armed cross within a circle and the X within a circle (for the higher note). Maybe one day we will create a new word for a person who has integrated both their yang and yin energies. You would then have men, women and a new word for both such as andron or something similar.

To come back to what the gridlines represent in our personal energy system, there are four horizontal lines that stand out in the energy field as well as one vertical line. The two slanted X lines are not all that often addressed, but they are no less important. When all is well the energy flow through the lines is smooth, but if there are any issues, there can be debris and blockages situated along them; they can look vague or askew; they can be congested; it can seem that small bits are missing or that one line is far more pronounced than the others. To those who are clairvoyant, the lines themselves look like misty bands of light.

The Yang Line

This vertical line runs through the whole person, from well over the head to below the feet, in the very centre of the body. This line represents our get up and go and how strong and confident we are in the world. There is only one of these lines that stands out and it runs along the spine.

The YIN Lines

The horizontal or Yin lines are as follows:

~The Shoulder Line~

This line runs through both shoulders (shoulder joints) along the collarbone. It represents how we take in new concepts, information or ideas and how we start to process these.

~The Integration Line~

This line runs horizontally through the body, along the bottom part of the solar plexus chakra but above the navel. It represents how we start to assimilate new concepts with the aim of using them in our life. If we straighten our arms next to our body, this line is in line with our elbows.

~The Hip Line~

This line runs horizontally through the hips, (hip joints) along the bottom part of the sacral chakra. It represents how we manifest and express our concepts in the world and make active use of them.

~The Knee Line~

This line runs horizontally along the knees. It represents what we do with great ease and is therefore often an indication that change is needed. This may be the case when we do our job without having to think and are not enthused or challenged any longer.

There is a line that runs along the ankles, but we do not include this in healing sessions since it relates to our grounding (and being part of the physical world). If we use healing tools these are placed underneath the feet and address this part automatically. In an energy healing session without the use of any tools, the grounding aspect of the session will do the same.

The Androgynous Lines

These two lines run from above each shoulder to below each hip. They cross over in the centre of the body somewhere between the heart and the sacral chakras. These lines represent stages and areas of life experiences that have been fully integrated or that are about to be mastered both from a yin and a yang perspective.

Almost all the lines cross or are situated near our major joints and it is interesting to note that joints are often out of kilter with regard to how we move through life experiences.

7

Additional Energy Centres and Subtle Layers

There are what can be termed 'bridges' between the seven main chakras, although some of these can be viewed as small centres in their own right. There are also energy centres, other than the crown, outside of the physical form. Healers usually focus on the main seven chakras, but at times it can be of benefit to address one or more of these 'additional' ones. To do this safely and responsibly, one must be highly proficient in assessing the subtle energy systems, and also intuiting how much clients are able to absorb safely during a healing session.

The Earth Chakra

This 'chakra' serves mainly as a point of reference. It is situated about one metre or so beneath the feet if standing, or the base of the spine if sitting on the ground. The colour vibration is a silvery black and it relates to a deep understanding of matter, crystals, minerals and metals as well as the connection between all that is in 'physical' form. It can also be used as a portal into 'the void'. Its main function relates to manifestation to deeper levels, manipulation of matter, more profound grounding into matter and the understanding of order and chaos. Some dysfunctions include a misuse of knowledge and power, practices of dark magic and use of this point of reference to link to unsavoury energies.

The Star Chakra

This 'chakra' is also a point of reference, situated about one metre above the crown chakra. The colour vibration is a luminous clear light with a tinge of the palest pink and golden inclusions. It relates to a higher link and the understanding (not just theoretical) that this brings. Its main function is the establishment of a more tangible link to the Angelic, the ability to channel what can be termed 'higher wisdom' and a profound archetypal comprehension. It is also associated with a deeper grasp of one's Soul purpose and being a positive co-creator of all that exists. The main dysfunctions are having doubts and fears concerning Light work and misdirection resulting in distortion of knowledge.

Both these 'chakras' are only relevant to those who have walked the path towards ever greater Light for quite some time, and who practise their increased awareness in daily life. For those who are not ready to incorporate such high energies, activating or working with these centres can result in major upheavals and imbalance. In advanced development groups, these points of reference are sometimes addressed, with the person on the receiving end being fully aware of what is going on, and then using the healing and group energy for their personal development. The healers in this case only hold the space.

Telepathic Chakra

This can be viewed as an energy centre, albeit of a little less importance than the brow centre. It is situated in the centre of the forehead, slightly more towards the hairline. The colour vibration is a night colour, (deeper than indigo), with a hint of deep purple. Its function is mainly telepathy; being aware of other people's thoughts. It is also about transcending time and space but with control of this. Prophetic abilities and continuity of consciousness are other functions. Some dysfunctions are when someone is too open or too much aware of other people's thought processes without boundaries or control. This chakra is forming in individuals who have reached a certain level of awareness with regard to their inner development. In most other people it serves as a bridge between the crown and brow.

Medullah Chakra

This centre is situated at the top of the spine. Some perceive it as the back of the brow chakra although it is also considered a centre in itself. The colour vibration is a deep electric blue. Apart from relating to most qualities of the brow centre, it is one of the places where energies of a more unpleasant nature tend to try to come in. When out of kilter, it can indicate the need to protect the whole system. Some of the dysfunctions are feeling vulnerable, psychic problems, stress issues and vertigo (with no medical reason).

Thymus Chakra

This centre is situated between the heart and throat chakras. The colour vibration is turquoise. It relates to the immune system and the chakras between which it is situated. Functions are communicating with a more open heart, being highly inspirational, and it also can help strengthen the auric field on levels that relate to this. Some of the dysfunctions are having few or no boundaries when in a stage of change, and an inability to integrate as well as express higher levels of being. This centre is becoming more apparent in many people and could be a sign that they are energetically evolving, thereby being able to reach a higher note.

Higher Solar Area

The higher solar area is situated just below the ribcage and the colour is an olive green. This small centre serves mainly as a bridge between the solar plexus and heart chakras. The only reason to address this 'centre', is to help facilitate movement between these two chakras if there is a blockage. Such a blockage is usually related to ordinary thought processes rather than more profound issues, when the movement is blocked from the solar plexus towards the heart chakra. If it is the other way around, it indicates that the individual is trying to act in a more loving and inclusive manner in the world.

Navel Chakra

This small centre is situated in the navel. The colour vibration is a pale orange tinged with gold. It relates to the bond with the birth mother as well as being nourished and nurtured. Another function is a remembering of coming into matter and this centre may be out of kilter in those who have had a difficult time in the womb or during birth. It can also relate to issues concerning dependence on others, especially blood family members. It has quite a strong connection to the thymus chakra although it mostly serves as a bridge between the solar plexus and the sacral chakras.

Some are of the opinion that there is also a small centre between the base and sacral chakras but I have not had much experience of this although one can bridge these two chakras energetically. If this is done from the sacral towards the base, it will be in relation to helping with manifesting plans, and the other way around can indicate the need to be a little more down to earth or solid with regard to certain sacral chakra qualities.

Hand Chakras

When channelling healing energies, these are also emitted via the palms of our hands, the centre of which are our hand chakras. Our fingertips also have tiny energy centres that emit a slightly finer and faster energy. Most of the time healers channel via their hand chakras although the energies also flow via one or more of the other chakras. Healers do not decide where the energies are emitted from – this occurs automatically.

Foot Chakras

We also have chakras that are situated at a mid-point at the soles of our feet. At times these can be blocked or full of debris which makes it a little more difficult to ground. Healers often clear or address these small centres, either for themselves or for their clients.

There are many more tiny chakras, but healers do not work directly on these, which is why they are not mentioned.

Layers Eight and Nine of the Auric Field

These two layers can be perceived as one layer only, since they relate to both the Earth and Star points of reference. One cannot actively address one of these without the other, since meditating on the Earth 'chakra', without being linked to the high frequencies of the Star 'chakra' is unwise, and when meditating on the Star 'chakra', one needs the depth of grounding of the Earth 'chakra'. These 'chakras', as well as the two extra layers around the auric field are, as mentioned earlier, for self-development and awareness only. The colour vibrations of these layers can be perceived as a velvet-like black with a luminous pearl and white golden sheen although this serves as a vague description only.

If there are any concerns in this layer, you must address these yourself, although in a group energy of those who are of a similar vibration, this can prove to be a little easier than going it alone. Issues of transcending space and time, becoming aware of far greater patterns of existence, matters pertaining to the soul and similar such topics relate to this subtle double layer. It is deeply personal and not for others to intrude on, even with the best intent.

8

How the Systems Interrelate

All the energy systems are interrelated and can ultimately affect our physical body. One example to illustrate how the energy systems interconnect, is when during a session a healer addresses a chakra, and suddenly debris or blockages appear in one or more of the subtle layers of the energy field, which were previously clear. In this case, addressing the chakra resulted in hidden mental, emotional, or other issues coming to the fore, which then showed up in related layers of the field. The healer would then need to respond accordingly. Another example of this is when one or two chakras are out of kilter, as well as a few of the gridlines. The healer would start by addressing the gridlines, and then perceive that the chakras in question were all of a sudden back in balance. One or two other ones, however, were now spinning out of balance and in need of work. This scenario demonstrates ones of the reasons why a healer has to constantly monitor what is occurring during a session. The whole field is in constant motion and what is addressed in one part, more often than not triggers something in another.

The chakra system itself is interconnected, which means that what occurs in one can hugely affect another. If one chakra is going through a major change, the one above or below will also be considerably affected and may therefore also need work. There are also chakras that are markedly related to others. The throat and sacral chakras, the heart and solar plexus chakras and the brow and base chakras are examples of this.

I mentioned the physical body, even if healers do not directly address this, because our energy systems ultimately also affect it. One example of this is an occasion when I received healing and flower remedies from a highly experienced healer. The session was great, but the next day I was in acute physical pain, to the point that I had to take some medication for it. The pain was around the scar of an operation I had around twenty years previously. With the pain I experienced a few intense unpleasant emotions. The next day the pain was gone and I felt fine. When I asked the healer about the flower remedy, the description of it mentioned scars, and I understood that I had experienced what is termed a healing crisis. It was obviously a huge release that also included part of my physical body. Another example is that when we experience something traumatic such as breaking a limb, this can have a big effect in parts of our energy field. It also shows how healing can support us through all life experiences.

I personally believe that all that occurs in our inner world, apart from fleeting issues, is ultimately expressed in our outer world. How this plays out depends on the quality of the continual processes in our energetic makeup.

An example to clarify this is the following scenario: someone has been very badly treated by a number of people and resents this. She or he cannot let go of these feelings, which over time intensify and ultimately become obsessive. If this is not dealt with, serious physical illness can result. Had this person received help, including that of a healer, the issue would have shown up in various parts of the energy field and been addressed accordingly. The person could have subsequently suffered from a nasty cold or something similar, in order to clear away any residue of this situation, rather than having to cope with a more serious illness. The issue is still expressed in the world, but in a less detrimental manner. The above may be a difficult concept to take on board initially, but it is worthwhile to look at your life and try to gauge if you can find similar, although hopefully less dramatic examples. As is mentioned several times in this book, only take in what you can relate to with regard to such concepts and put the rest aside.

9

Assessing the State of the Subtle Energy Systems

It can be counterproductive, when initially learning about subtle anatomy and healing, to focus on what each of the systems represent and the various qualities they relate to when assessing someone else, because this can lead to an incorrect way of working. If a client communicates to a healer what is going on in his/her life, the healer will obviously listen and create a safe space for the client to be able to do this. However, healers cannot offer any advice to clients concerning their personal issues, nor use such information to determine which areas in their energy field must be addressed. Instead, after the relaxation process, they must focus exclusively on and evaluate the actual state of their clients' subtle anatomy and, according to their findings, establish where to start working and which tools to use.

The theory about what the energy systems represent is, however, highly relevant for healers with regard to understanding what is involved in their work, as well as their personal healing and development processes. The paradox is that almost none of this knowledge is used in healing others.

You can assess your own energy field and the systems within it by linking to the Light and your guidance, and then entering a meditative state. Once you have established what is out of kilter, you can do a number of self-healing exercises.

To assess a client, you first (re) link to the Light and then to the client, which includes his/her Higher Self. You then take the client through a relaxation process, after which you look at the energy field using your inner vision. Your attention may be drawn to the state of the chakras and/or gridlines, or to what is occurring in various layers of the subtle energy field. You will also have gained an initial impression of the client's overall energy during your initial chat, and with all this information can then decide on how to proceed. If you are in doubt about anything, step back for a moment, re-link and start again.

Assessing Chakras

Where chakras are concerned, healers will assess the state of a client's chakra system and then, according to findings, work where indicated or choose appropriate crystals to help bring the system back into the best possible balance. This is not all that easy, because chakras cannot be perceived with the naked eye and, since each person has different life experiences, one cannot possibly generalise.

Even if a client states that they have an issue that seems to relate to a specific chakra, the chakra in question could well be in balance, and the cause of the issue situated in a different part or parts of the energy field. If using crystals or other healing tools, the choice of these must always relate to the actual states of the chakras that are being addressed, and not to physical, emotional, mental or spiritual traits that a client has expressed. They must also relate to the overall energetic makeup of the client.

The way to learn to assess the state of chakras is through practice, practice and more practice. Those who are starting out, sometimes use a pendulum, but after a year or so of experience, this is then replaced by intuition. Some perceive the chakras with their inner eye, some sense their state by gently holding their hand over them and those more experienced instantly know the state of the chakras, the moment they focus on a client's energy systems at the start of a session. Healers must be able to evaluate if a chakra is spinning too fast (over-active), spinning too slowly (under-active), too open or blocked and to what degree. They also need to know if a chakra is damaged or traumatised, since they then would not work on it, unless highly experienced. If a chakra is in acute change, advanced techniques may be appropriate. Healers also need to know when the system is in relative balance.

Assessing chakras with a pendulum is done when fully linked to both the Light and your client. Working with a pendulum is a way of making your own intuition visible and is not influenced or controlled by any form of guidance. To use this method, you must first establish how the pendulum can show up various chakra states. Do this by choosing a number of different swings the pendulum can make. It can swing in a round circle (of various sizes) which can be in a clockwise or counter-clockwise direction. The pendulum can also swing in a vertical, horizontal or slanted fashion. It can swing in an irregular manner or stay motionless. You can relate specific movements of your pendulum to the various different states chakras can express, and then memorize which is which.

Please note that you must not swing a pendulum directly over a chakra, since this can be highly disruptive or unpleasant for a sensitive person, to the point that they may start to feel dizzy or nauseous. The way to assess is to first ask to perceive the state of the chakra system. You then hold one hand over each chakra in turn and look at and remember the swing of the pendulum that you hold in your other hand (away from the body of the client). Remove your hand briefly between each chakra in order to keep their energies contained. The whole assessment process is fast because you only need a few swings of the pendulum to see what state a chakra expresses. If the chakras are in relative balance, they will all have an identical swing (of the same size and speed). Although most healers do not use this method after a year or so of training, it is still useful should there ever be any doubt.

There are healers who are able to assess chakras in far more detail and perceive on which specific level there may be an issue (there are approximately seven levels in each chakra). Such highly intuitive folk can also determine in which 'direction' the chakra is out of kilter. Not many can (as yet) work with such precision, and it is more than sufficient to just establish how a chakra is out of balance if tools such as crystals are used. Most healers, however, can evaluate in which of the various gateways the imbalance in a chakra is most acute. Once profound healing work becomes better known, more healers will delve deeper and will then hopefully also be supported by science or at least quantum physics.

Assessing Subtle Bodies

Assessing the state of the subtle layers in the energy field is far less complicated than assessing the state of chakras, and is also learned via practice. Many healers do this by touch, others perceive the layers with their inner eye, and then there are those who instantly know where to work. There are usually several blockages in one or more layers of the field. Some of these are easy to clear, others can be quite stubborn. Most people usually have something going on in the second and third layers since these relate to our emotional as well as thought processes. As indicated earlier, when chakras are being addressed, this often has an impact on the other systems, therefore, even if the layers seem in relative balance at first, once a healing session proceeds, the state of the field may suddenly change. This is why a healer assesses at the start and also a few times during a healing session.

Assessing Gridlines

The easiest way to assess the gridlines is by standing at the feet of a client and using your inner eye. Some perceive them as misty bands of light, others can sense them by touch and then there are those who instantly know the state of this system when they focus on it. Lines can be clogged, too faint, wavy, or parts can seem to be missing. They usually need to be cleared of 'debris', straightened, strengthened to various degrees or somewhat re-defined in rare cases.

Assessing the Auric Field as a Whole

This is done intuitively whilst gaining an overall impression of the client when they come in, speak to you and during the relaxation process at the start of a session. You then 'look' at the whole field for just an instant. The main reason for this is to gauge the extent of energy a client can handle and, more importantly, if using tools such as crystals or flowers, to make sure you do not 'overdo' things. In order to be able to assess the auric field as a whole, you must be attuned to the Light prior to a client coming to you. Do, however, not link to clients before they are with you, since this may disorientate them and there is no need for this since our energy field is in constant change.

10

Energy Healing

An energy healing session is relatively straightforward. Once the client is comfortable and relaxed, the healer will establish where in the energy field there is an imbalance and address this accordingly. Most healers start with the chakra system and channel energy into those that need it, either at the front or the back or, if the client is sitting, both at the front and the back simultaneously. It is not recommended to channel energy into chakras too close to the physical body because blockages or any other form of imbalance tend to be situated a little further afield.

Once all chakras are restored to the best possible balance, the healer will connect them before proceeding to address various layers of the field. This is done by placing one hand at the base of the spine and one at the top of the spine and then briefly channelling Light into these areas on the etheric level of the energy field. They will also evaluate if any of the subtle layers or one or more of the gridlines need work, and after this clear the field and ground themselves and the client. Depending on what is occurring in the client's life, one or more sessions may be necessary. The norm is that three sessions, which must be at least one week apart, are usually sufficient.

Channelling beneficial energies into a person's energy field, and the systems within this field, affects each individual differently. No two people are the same with regard to what they are experiencing in their life and what their energy systems represent. While one can say that all human beings are similar on physical levels, looking at this in a holistic manner is a very different story, and shows that we are the most complicated species that walk this earth. The reason that each of us is so special is that each of us is unique. As mentioned previously, healing energies support an individual rather than fix issues, and it is worthwhile to look at how this can happen on various levels of the energy field.

Energy healers rarely work on etheric levels other than to help infuse this layer with energy if it is depleted. They can also help activate and stimulate natural healing processes in emergencies or ease pain in some cases. On emotional levels, after having received healing, feelings may intensify for a few days, so the client can become aware of what is going on and take steps to move through issues. When too many issues come to the fore, it may be necessary for a client to get additional help from someone proficient in a listening therapy such as counselling. Counselling can be a valuable therapy when you are going through a difficult patch in your life. It is my understanding, however, that if this is combined with healing, people are able to move with far more ease through the whole process. Counselling will enable the client to work through their issues and the healer will address what shows up in the energy field, which can also be on other levels than just the mental and emotional. Many VHF graduates are also trained counsellors, and they agree with this notion.

When a healer addresses the lower mental levels, thought processes that a client is not aware of may come to the fore, forgotten memories of difficult experiences can suddenly emerge or insights may be gained to help resolve issues. This level of our energy field is rarely in balance, because we think during every waking moment, and our thoughts are not always of a helpful nature. As mentioned earlier, the lower mental level also includes what is stored in our subconscious mind, and blockages in that area can also show up during or after a healing session so they can be subsequently dealt with.

When higher mental levels are addressed, lack of inspiration may be assisted or a greater appreciation of beauty and harmony promoted. Issues regarding compassion and nurturing also pertain to this area, and those involved in the arts often need attention here.

On causal levels, memories from early childhood or other lifetimes, but always relating to what needs to be addressed, may come to light. Since this level is associated with our blueprint, it interpenetrates our whole system. Some of our thought processes, emotional responses, inherent talents, beliefs and even physical traits can relate to experiences from other lifetimes.

Spiritual levels are usually addressed with clients who are becoming more aware of the worlds of energy, and those who are interested in philosophy, religious teachings or similar subjects. Issues in these levels also tend to show up in dire and sometimes life-threatening situations.

Since chakras represent many different qualities which are more distinctive than those in the subtle layers, addressing these is a far more intricate process and can therefore be quite invasive. As mentioned earlier, each chakra relates to a considerable number of specific life experiences and how we respond to these. If you think about how many different experiences life can offer, and of the many levels these experiences contain, it becomes obvious that a healer can only work to the point of greatest need at any one time. Although all the energy centres can be addressed, it is important to take special care with the crown chakra, since this represents a person's link with the Light. Unless there are special circumstances, healers only briefly touch on that area. For a sensitive person it can be very unpleasant to have a healer channel there for longer than a moment.

The gridlines are far more general, because they relate to how we tend to move through life and how we integrate whatever is going on, but they are no less important. Addressing blockages in these lines, or strengthening them, can help us move forward and get on with everything with more ease. One can see this especially with regard to both the knee and the shoulder lines. These relate to change, which is something so many of us find difficult and often try to avoid!

There are those who believe that healing requires a set procedure, which must be followed regardless of what is going on in a client's energy field. I personally do not agree with this, since channelling energies into a chakra that does not need this risks unbalancing it. Channelling into the auric field where this is not required can over-stimulate this part of the subtle anatomy and what it represents, and the same goes for the gridlines. This is why we advise to only channel energies where required.

There are healers who believe that the Angelic takes care of where healing energies are supposed to go during a session. They sit near a client, link and then channel the energies towards him/her in general. This notion is correct, but only suitable for clients who are extremely fragile, very young, very old or in the process of dying. For most other people this procedure is not as effective as a session where the healer addresses issues in the energy field directly. The main reason for this is that as human beings we must take as much responsibility for our actions as possible, which includes facilitating a healing session. If a healer can do it, there is no need for an Angelic being to intervene and in the world of energy nothing is done unnecessarily

However, sometimes, when a session is almost over, it can be appropriate to sit near a client and re-link to the highest level you can reach and again ask to be given what is in accordance with the client's highest good. You then let the energies flow towards the client's auric field as a whole. Sometimes a great deal of energy is given, other times none. You would do this after you cleared the energy field for the last time, but before the grounding process. I personally only do this when I receive a strong indication near the end of a session that a client requires it, and am usually given relevant feedback by the client after the session has finished.

Although energy healing by itself is much easier to learn than crystal healing, most long-standing energy healing organisations deem that it also takes two years before one is ready to practise professionally. The main reasons for this are the need for supervised practice as well as intuitive and inner development. Hands-on experience and working in a group energy are as valuable with regard to energy healing only, as they are with regard to crystal healing. Being part of a group of healers generates far more energy than working alone, and makes it easier to experience and perceive what occurs within one's own and others' energy fields during a healing session or in meditation. Equally in a group, provided it is not too large, all participants learn from each other.

Hazards

It is important to be aware of certain hazards relating to energy work in order to help avoid these with respect to both healers and clients.

Healers are advised not to practise when unwell, tired, if they are under acute stress or dealing with too many difficult life experiences. They could inadvertently transmit such energies to their clients or, alternatively, take on clients' issues. Therefore, only practise when you have a strong energy field and are able to link and channel properly.

Always be as measured as possible, especially with those who have fragile energy fields. You do not wish to trigger a huge healing crisis.

If at all possible, refrain from practising professionally on close family members, including your children. The reason for this is that most of us are unable to detach personally from someone we love. We cannot then avoid projecting our own opinions about them and therefore fail to perceive clearly what is going on in their energy field. There are instances when you cannot avoid giving healing to loved ones and then it is best to try to stay detached or, if that is difficult, imagine you are giving healing to someone you do not know!

If working with small children in a hospital, please make sure you strengthen your energy field as much as possible. We cannot help but want to give our personal energy to little ones who are suffering, which is not as helpful as channelling healing energies only. Being aware of this is usually sufficient, so you can be warm, compassionate and friendly without compromising on your link and channelling. Please also note that the Angelic is always very much present in healing work with children.

When assessing what is going on with clients, some healers often feel within themselves what their clients are suffering from, including if they have physical symptoms. This is not healthy, because there is then a great risk of taking on such issues. I strongly advise that if this is the case with you, you take steps to strengthen your energy field and always ensure you evaluate in a different manner. Even if the sensations are only slight, it is not necessary to work in this way. It can indicate that you have a great deal of compassion for others, but in the end, your own health is as important as that of your clients!

11

Colour, Sound and Healing

Healers must have a certain level of colour awareness since colour affects us considerably. This awareness is, however, not to be confused with colour therapy, which is a therapy in its own right and requires a different skill set from energy healing.

Colour is the visible part of the electromagnetic spectrum and is white light split into seven spectrum colours. Colour moves in wave forms through the universe and the longer or slower waves are visible to us as red, and the faster ones as violet. You can clearly see this in a rainbow although the colours of the rainbow are a little more radiant than those in the physical world. It is interesting to note that in meditation the colours we sometimes see are also more luminous. Most people who start out in meditation will at some point perceive a purple colour behind their third eye, which is far more vibrant than any purple material on the physical plane.

We take in colour via our eyes, skin and energy field and also ingest it in the foods we eat. Colour vibrations affect living tissue and a life without colour is unthinkable!

Unlike colour therapists, healers do not choose specific colours they channel, although they may be aware of a lack of a certain colour in a client's energy field. If this happens at the very start of a session, they may mention this colour in the initial relaxation process, so the client can focus on it. Healers also often notice dark or murky colours in certain layers of an energy field and then take extra care to address this. They can also become aware of a colour vibration that they are channelling and then let the client know this after the session has finished. The client may then choose to incorporate that colour into his or her daily life for a while by wearing relevant clothes, buying relevant flowers to look at or by meditating. Meditating whilst focussing on a specific colour combines thought and colour vibrations, which will affect the energy field accordingly. A few colour vibrations and their main qualities are mentioned here.

Red is a warming and stimulating colour. It can be of benefit if there is a lack of stamina, passion, motivation or vitality. It also represents power and action. It can help with grounding, self-confidence and a lack of purpose.

Orange is a joyful and uplifting vibration. It also represents self-respect, practicality, creativity, cheerfulness and spontaneity. It can act as a tonic for a feeling of jadedness.

Yellow is also about joy and happiness. It is the colour of sunshine and high energy and if you feel a little depressed this colour will help to lift your mood. It relates to both the mind and the ego and therefore also to concentration, will and self-worth. The colour gold is more about wisdom.

Green is the colour of nature, balance and relaxation. It is a stabilising colour and is also about harmony, self-love, empathy and abundance. Many relate it to the release of tensions and stress.

Pink is the colour of unconditional love, compassion, gentleness, nurturing, kindness, softness and openness. It is also about giving and receiving and can act as a countermeasure to rage and anger.

Blue soothes and calms. It is about peace, loyalty, hope, honesty and communication. It also relates to the qualities of self-expression, truth and healing. It is one of the colours that can help with relaxation and stress-release.

Indigo relates to responsibility, understanding, profound wisdom, vision and high ideals. It is often effective in counteracting pain and releasing of tensions. It is protective and is the colour of the seeker.

Violet is about dignity, transformation, insights and inspiration. It is a cleanser of negativity and relates to spiritual growth and service. It is also a colour of power but more in the way of inner authority than of action.

Turquoise is a protective colour in the way that it strengthens and replenishes. It also helps with clarity of expression and encourages communication. It is very much a 'feel good' colour.

Black absorbs light and is about stability and security. It can drain excess energy, relieve pain and help with grounding. It also represents power, but in the way of mastery and it can reveal the hidden. It has a quality of protection, but only for those who have overcome most of their fears or other shadow issues.

White reflects light and is about purity, clarity and perfection. It contains all colours and is often perceived as the colour of the initiate. It is one of the colours that can help clear negativity.

These few colours and their basic qualities, mainly serve as a tool for awareness and self-healing for an energy healer. For those who wish to use it to a greater extent in their energy work it is recommended to attend a colour therapy course.

Colour Exercise

For this exercise you need a set of seven different brightly coloured scarves consisting of bright red, orange, yellow, green, light blue, indigo and purple. You could also add an extra scarf of turquoise. Place the scarves on the floor in front of you, choose the one you like most and focus on it. Imagine that you are taking in that colour throughout your energy field, using the breath. Just be aware that the bright red and orange must not be directed into chakras, other than the base and sacral or further than the emotional layer of the auric field. The other colours can go anywhere. If you feel you still need more of that colour, pick up the scarf and drape it around your body. You will be surprised how effective this is if you feel a little low in energy. Most people need to do the exercise with two or three different colours before they feel balanced and energized.

Sound and Healing

Working consciously with sound is extremely powerful, since we respond to sound vibrations on every level of our being, including our physical body. An awareness of how to use sound in healing is not to be confused with sound therapy, which is a separate therapy and requires lengthy training. In healing work, sound is important with regard to the tone of your voice and the use of Tibetan bowls, chimes or Ting Sha, all of which are easy to learn and implement.

The tone of a voice is highly revealing. The reason that parents usually know when their child is fibbing is not necessarily because they are psychic; it is because the tone of the child's voice will be slightly off-key. The same goes for long-term relationships; one almost always knows when a partner is hiding something, because there will be an uneasy feeling, caused by the tone of voice. When you are linked to the Light and carefully listen to a client, their voice can also give you an insight into what is going on in their energy field. Psychics or mediums who give readings always ask their clients to say something. This is not in order to glean information; it is to tune in to the sound of their voice. It is obviously equally important that a healer's voice is of a good note, since most people will instinctively pick up on anything that is off-key, especially when in a state of profound relaxation and deeper awareness.

Healers mainly use their voice during the relaxation process or if an active healing meditation forms part of the session. They can, however, also gently chant a note into their client's auric field if this is appropriate. This is quite a powerful technique and should only be used if the healer is highly confident in doing this. In my experience, out of a class of ten graduates, not more than two or three use this technique frequently. You can also use vowel sounds for self-healing purposes which is covered in a later chapter.

Most healers use a Tibetan bowl in order to help clear or energize a client's energy field. With sound, it is important to have the correct intent, so if clearing someone's energy field, the focus must be on clearing (for the highest good of the client) whilst doing this. An exercise describing how to do this is at the end of this chapter. At times, so much is being cleared that it is necessary to also replenish the resulting void, which can then be filled with healing energies. If using sound for this, the focus must be on replenishing the field.

Ting Sha are Tibetan bells that emit a sharp, high-pitched sound, which is not ideal to use during a healing session, because this could disturb a client who is in a state of deep relaxation. They are therefore mainly utilized to clear crystals or spaces and the same goes for chimes. You can, however, very softly tap a chime and draw it through an exceptionally grubby layer of a client's auric field.

Tuning forks must be used with great care since they are sine tones, which means they do not emit harmonics. They must also have the correct pitch, and in my personal view should not be used on chakras since the sound is too 'one pointed', intense and invasive. If a chakra needs such heavy duty clearing or energising, briefly sounding a Tibetan bowl over it is a better option. The sound of such a bowl emits harmonics, which will ensure that the appropriate levels within the chakra in question are reached. Tuning forks are, however, highly effective for use in meditation, and I usually advise students to obtain one or two for their own self-healing and development processes. I was advised many years ago by a highly respected and well-known expert in the field of sound and colour healing, that tuning forks that carry the old Viennese concert pitch are the best ones to use.

Many healers use rattles, drums and even didgeridoos, but as far as I am aware it is mainly Shamanic folk who do this, and since I do not have personal experience with these instruments, I cannot advise on them. I have, however, been told by a number of people that such healing work is highly effective, including on more physical levels. There are also sound healers who use gongs to give their clients a 'sound bath', which has been reported to be highly beneficial. If you need to clear a large space, a gong is of course the best instrument you could possibly use!

A self-healing sound exercise is to enter a meditative state and listen to an Audio CD created by Joachim-Ernst Berend, also the author of Nada Brahma, the World is Sound. He created a number of CDs that depict the sound of the planets, including that of the Earth. A much higher octave of the Earth sound frequency translates into an orange red, a little like terra cotta, which represents the colour vibration of our planet. Meditating with this sound connects you deeply to the vibration of the Earth and if you then hold a crystal such as Carnelian or Red Jasper, this will intensify the experience.

Sound Clearing Exercise

The clearing exercise with a Tibetan bowl is as follows. If a person is sitting or standing, ping the bowl and take it from the top (slightly on the side and not over the crown

chakra) of the head down to the ground. Do this on the left and right side and also the front and the back of the person, not too close to the body. Focus on clearing the field whilst doing this. If the person is lying down, you do the left and right side and the front twice. The second time you just imagine that you are addressing the back. Energy follows thought so this will happen.
For yourself you can sit down and use the same method.

12

Flowers and Healing

Flowers are wonderful to use in combination with energy healing. Their energy is more subtle than that of crystals, but no less potent. Introducing flowers in or around someone's energy field during a healing session can have a profound effect, so please tread with care. The reason for flowers being such amazing healing tools could be that they represent the highest aspect of the plant kingdom, which in itself is a 'finer' vibration than the mineral kingdom. Order and beauty are two important principles with regard to our existence and both relate to crystals and flowers. One could say that in crystals order comes before beauty and in flowers it is the other way around, and their energy is also more ethereal. Reaching deep blockages often requires a more subtle approach and flowers are then often suitable. I also find that flowers help to create an instant link to the Angelic.

Flowers can be placed anywhere in the energy field, provided bright red and orange coloured flowers are not used on the higher chakras or higher levels. They relate especially well to the emotional, higher mental and spiritual levels of the auric field. When flowers form part of a session, they are, like crystals, tuned for the highest good of that client. On courses when flower healing is practised, I usually keep the flowers that were used on the students. Some of these last for many days, others for a few hours only, which shows that they keep working on the person until no longer needed. I once kept a flower used for healing in a small vase and it lasted for more than a month!

Plants can be used to assist with the grounding process, by placing them beneath the feet of a client, and a stem with leaves is helpful to clear an auric field. Drawing a flower through someone's energy field, not only helps to clear it of debris, but also infuses it with a specific vibration. A healer always knows when to use flowers or plants during a healing session, because s/he will become aware of the need for this via a strong and immediate thought. When this occurs, a suitable flower or plant is always available. Flowers can also be used in combination with crystal healing when crystals are appropriate but a more subtle approach is needed for parts of the energy field. Please always check for allergies before using flowers on a client.

It is advisable not to use herbs in the auric field, unless one is both an experienced herbalist and healer. Herbs are special plants that act like medicine and their energy is extremely potent. Herbalism is considered a therapy within itself. There are many people who grow herbs in their gardens, patios or even on their windowsills. Herbs must be pruned often and placing a vase of herbs in your home and tuning them for your (and everyone else's) well-being is fine, as long as nobody is allergic to any of these! Herbs were used frequently in more ancient times, until the unfortunate persecution of witches reared its ugly head, and those who were knowledgeable in this field had to hide or stop practising altogether.

Flower Essences

Flower essences, especially Bach Flower essences, have been well known for nearly a century and are also considered a separate therapy. They can, however, be used in combination with crystal and energy healing, if a healer is qualified to do so, and has additional expertise in applying them directly into the energy field. Flower essences work by flooding the energy field, especially the emotional layer of the auric field, with positive qualities, opposing specific negative ones from which a person may be suffering. Some of the essences also relate well to other layers of the field, most notably the lower mental, causal and spiritual levels.

There are 38 Bach Flower essences plus one that is made up of five of these, and which is the well-known Rescue remedy or Five Flower essence. The way essences are made is that suitable flowers are picked and placed in water and sunlight for a few hours or, alternatively, boiled in water. The essences are then placed in small stock bottles and topped with brandy in order to keep them fresh.

Many healers have a box of all the essences and use them for self-healing purposes. The ones that are used especially often are Crab Apple, which is the cleansing remedy, Clematis which helps with the grounding process and Walnut which is excellent for strengthening the energy field when undergoing some form of change. Star of Bethlehem is used to help with shock and grief, Mimulus for known fears and Aspen for nightmares. The reason these essences are mentioned in this book is to make the reader aware of them. To cover this subject in more depth would require a separate book.

13

The Elements

Everything in nature, including our physical body, is made up of the four elements which are air, fire, water and earth. There is also a fifth element called ether, which represents the energies behind nature and is the domain of the Devic kingdom which consists of all the nature spirits. This view has been held as fact for thousands of years by Druids, Wiccans, healers and similar people; although in our current world it has been replaced by atomic theory and the idea that matter and energy are interchangeable. It can, however, not be disputed that in order to keep our body alive and functioning we have to eat, drink, breathe and we also need light. All of this is provided by and via the elements.

The Angelic is in overall charge of nature which is why it follows that having a physical body indicates that we have a direct link to this kingdom. Some view this link as their Guardian Angel, others perceive it more as nature itself and the elements are obviously hugely important for our health on both physical and energetic levels.

On down-to-earth levels, Human beings were and still are supposed to take good care of nature but unfortunately, we are not doing our job all that well. The elements of earth, water, air and even the space around us have become increasingly toxic and harmful to all of us, as well as nature itself. We cannot avoid being negatively affected by toxins and it is therefore important to try to live as healthily as possible, including having a balanced diet, detoxing when necessary, exercising and so on, which is not within the remit of this book. We can, however, indicate what can be done on energetic levels.

The element of earth relates to being well-grounded, the ability to manifest and being practical. A lack of earth can result in not being able to realise one's plans. It can also show up as being vague or disinterested in what is going on, or day dreaming most of the time. It is not for nothing that a down-to-earth quality in a person, which includes being sensible and practical, is admired so much. Where healers are concerned; a lack of earth can result in not being able to ground the healing energies to the lower levels of the energy field. This element relates most to the Earth itself.

With regard to inner development, a lack of earth can indicate an inclination to follow the path of the mystic rather than the occultist (to use old-fashioned terminology). The mystic's aim is to reach and then join the highest Light vibrations, and such individuals often retreat from the world. The occultist aims to bring Light into the world and is actively doing this in day-to-day life, which requires a strong link to the Earth. Healers are usually a mixture of these two types, although most lean a little more strongly to one of them. The Devic energies behind this element are named Gnomes and the chakra it relates most to is the base.

The element of water represents our emotional nature and being able to 'go with the flow' when necessary. A lack of water relates to repressing or ignoring your feelings and therefore being a little stoic. This can result in difficult feelings building up over time and then affecting you in a detrimental fashion. Too much water can lead to being somewhat over-emotional and not being able to plan, structure or manifest with ease. Like our bodies, the Earth itself is made up of more than seventy percent of water, which is constantly recycled!

The Devic beings behind this element are named Undines. Every lake, stream, pond, well, river, sea and ocean, is guarded by an Undine. If you sit quietly near a body of water and link, you will be able to sense such energies. The amazing book Messages from Water, written by Masaru Emoto, a Japanese doctor of alternative medicine, is a worthwhile read on the subject. This element relates strongly to the Moon and also predominantly to our sacral chakra.

The element of fire represents our levels of energy, passion, get up and go and enthusiasm. A lack of it can result in apathy or listlessness, also leading to having no incentive to do anything. Too much of this element can result in being overly aggressive, over enthusiastic, out of control and prone to burn out. This element also relates to our fight and flight response. Without the element of fire, we are not be able to function in this world, and it is of interest to note that those that are severely ill demonstrate an utter lack of it. The Devic energies behind this element are named Salamanders.

In Greek mythology the Titan Prometheus stole fire from the gods and gave this to humanity. He was punished for this by Zeus, the leader of the gods, who had him tied to a rock and instructed an eagle to eat his liver, which grew back every day. This went on for many years until Hercules, one of the heroes in Greek mythology, freed him. The liver relates to the solar plexus, which in turn relates to the element of fire. It also relates to the Sun.

The element of air relates to focus, concentration and thought processes. Too much air can result in obsession, overly thinking, being too much in one's head and so on. A lack of air can lead to stagnation and what is known as a grasshopper mentality. It can also lead to depression and not being able to formulate any plans or projects. The (probably) politically incorrect term 'airhead' is what an individual with an imbalance in this element used to be called. The Devic energies behind this element are named Sylphs.

We cannot survive without air for more than a few minutes and breathing correctly is one of the keys to health and well-being. Many of us breathe superficially, not filling the whole of our lungs with air on the in-breath, or fully emptying them on the out-breath. Nowadays there are short courses available on how to breathe properly and most yoga classes include this subject. Such courses are worthwhile attending if you find it difficult to change your habit of shallow breathing. This element loosely relates to the heart chakra, but more in the way of higher mental and inspirational thought processes.

The element of ether mainly relates to our vitality or lack of it. It also relates to all the energies behind nature such as the Devic and Angelic kingdoms, and is a link to these. I also relate this element to what is termed our Guardian Angel, who is our first and foremost link to the rest of the Angelic kingdoms. I do not believe we can have too much of this element, although a lack of it indicates that all is not well with us on physical levels. It has been reported by those who can perceive this layer around people that it vanishes shortly before we leave this Earth. The guardians of this element (and ultimately all the others) are the Angels.

It is definitely advisable to start using your ability to link and channel energies in relation to the elements. You can bless your food and water by briefly channelling energy into it. Also ensure that you are exposed to enough sunlight (in a safe manner). If you are intuitive, you will be aware of tiny sparks of Light in the air around you when you are in nature. Taking a few deep breaths whilst focussing on breathing these sparks into the area where your spleen is situated, will help energize you. Above all, ensure that the elements within you are as balanced as possible.

14

Inner Development

Starting out on the path of healing opens up a whole new world. This can be likened to an awe-inspiring adventure that is not only exciting, but also everlasting. In the beginning, it may be a little difficult to find one's way and not be distracted by some of the glitz of New Age practices, but the serious seeker will always find the right person at the right time to help him or her along. In the past, this used to be a guru or eminent leader of groups of people, and much of it was done in secret. However, this has changed dramatically over the last few decades.

Most profound healer training is done in small groups, and those who facilitate these rarely set themselves up as gurus. Although a tutor will teach the student how to facilitate healing and also how to use certain tools and techniques, s/he can only share personal truth with regard to development. The worlds of energy are immeasurable, and raising one's vibration is a never-ending process, not just relating to the world we live in. It is, therefore, up to the student to choose whether to take concepts on board or to put them aside. The path towards ever greater Light, love, truth and harmony is unique and personal for each of us, regardless of race, nationality, religion, belief system or orientation. There are also many different avenues to explore it, both in Eastern and Western traditions, although all of these involve profound inner growth and awareness in practice.

All human beings are on this journey towards Light even if many are not aware of it. Healers travel it consciously, and thereby accelerate their development. By linking to and channelling Light energies, that which is of a lower note always comes to the fore, which is why healer training is not always easy. It can be a road of trials and tribulations, and it is not for nothing that it is often called 'the razor-edged path'. It is, however, also incredibly rewarding and, rather than taking detours, it is worthwhile to try to stay on the straight and narrow. Lower notes can include difficult memories from childhood or even other lives. Feelings of hurt, anger, betrayal and anything of a similar nature may emerge in order to be dealt with, so the healer can move forward and integrate a higher note.

For those who have had a traumatic past, it may be necessary to seek help from a counsellor or similar practitioner for a while, in order to address thorny issues that come up. Ultimately every healer will come to the conclusion that s/he can take responsibility for almost everything that occurs in his/her personal life, be this in order to change something, learn a lesson or let go of the past. This can be hugely challenging, which is why it is helpful to have a few fellow traveller friends or colleagues to be able to share experiences with.

There is also a huge amount of joy on this path. It is wonderful to have the ability to help others, to be able to perceive more beauty and Light and to become more empowered rather than a victim of fate. Communicating with beings who take care of nature and other unseen energies is exciting, and finding one's place and purpose in this world on deeper levels is an incredible benefit. It is my perception that even if half of the world's population gained a basic awareness of this path, and then made an effort to address the lower vibrations in their energetic makeup, everything would change instantly for the better for everyone, including the health of the planet itself.

One trait we all exhibit without exception is projection, although most of us are unaware of it. Projection refers to unconsciously taking any unwanted emotions or personal characteristics that you possess, and attributing them to someone else. This can be done with both positive and negative feelings, and we mainly do it with any part of ourselves that we do not want to 'own'. The key to knowing if you are projecting is your emotions. If you are greatly disturbed and feel strongly about an issue you perceive as arising from another, there is usually a lesson you can learn about yourself. This does not mean that bad things should be ignored or readily absorbed because we do not always project; it is just a matter of self-evaluation.

Take the issue of bullying, which all of us find highly offensive. If you feel exceptionally upset when you read a story about bullying in a newspaper, this does not necessarily mean that you are a bully. It could be that you have felt or been bullied in the past, or that you are in the process of opening your heart centre a little more, in order to deepen levels of compassion. Bullying is horrible, but many bullies have been victims of this themselves. It must never be tolerated and if at all possible eradicated, but hatred for the perpetrator, although understandable, will have to be released in order to move forward and not give the bully any further power. If you realise what it is you needed to learn, and you subsequently read a story about bullying, you will then be able to acknowledge it without excessive emotion and upset, and treat it as information. This does not mean that you will become hard or unfeeling; you are merely changing the quality of sympathy for true compassion.

On the positive side, if you admire someone with all your heart and feel their qualities are remarkable, you probably have some of those same qualities yourself or are in the process of acquiring them. It is worth considering who you truly look up to and approve of, and you could discover that you have a lot in common! Another way to help address possible issues, is to look at the world as a mirror and take everything as a message of some sort, both the good and the bad! Equally, if anyone pushes your buttons excessively, it could be an indication that what they say is highly relevant to you, or that whatever you dislike about them is a quality you yourself may need to address. If you are stuck and unsure how to move forward, you can ask for a message, be this from the Light or your guidance, and then observe your surroundings where clues may become apparent.

Every single person you meet has importance and can be viewed as having a message for you. We are all interlinked, and in a certain sense, can be perceived as one great whole. My favourite analogy for this is the proverbial drop in the ocean of life. You are only one drop, but you can link to every other drop, be it polluted or clean. Even on physical levels, we are all linked; we only need to think of the element of water to realise this. There is a finite amount of water on this Earth which is constantly recycled. It may be unsettling to reflect upon this, but it flows through each and every one of us, and throughout the kingdoms of nature, connecting us all.

Unless you have chosen to retreat somewhere and live a quiet life, it can be a little testing to keep a balance between daily life and the amazing worlds of energy. The best way to deal with being in both worlds is to stay grounded and set a strong boundary when you are in the presence of people who may not be aware of or able to understand the worlds of energy. You can always do your energy work in private. On the other hand, you should avoid getting too caught up in the higher vibrations, and ensure you always use your awareness and insights to take action and bring about positive change. This can be done through your healing work, or you may be called to share your newfound knowledge with others. If so, always come from a point of experience rather than theory alone.

Personally, if I cannot actively use information from the Light, guidance, fellow humans or books, I put it aside.

Your world will change considerably when you step consciously onto this path and you may find that you also gain a whole new group of friends and acquaintances.

15

Cause and Effect

Everything we do, say, strongly think and feel has an effect on everything and everyone. This can be small, significant or huge, and it can be positive, negative or even both, depending on the circumstances. I have heard that one of the edicts of the Wiccan tradition is 'Do what you will as long as you do not harm anyone', or something along those lines. I do not think this is possible because our best intentions and actions can turn out to have disastrous results, and some of our errors can have beneficial effects. We cannot possibly see the bigger picture and, therefore, can only endeavour to come from the point of our highest truth and motivation at all times. At least we will then know that we could not have done 'better' and whichever of our actions we are not happy about, then become a learning curve.

Another point, already mentioned, is that everything we give out, both 'good' and 'bad', will at some stage return to us and is known as our karma. This may occur in our present incarnation or in another life and represents nothing but learning lessons while moving forward on the path towards enlightenment. Nobody can perceive their complete, personal karmic history, let alone envisage someone else's. It is too vast a subject, with too many implications, since our actions from this and other lifetimes will have affected millions of people as well as the planet itself.

Balancing karma is also not a matter of being judged by a higher authority, and then punished or rewarded accordingly. Many of those who practise profound inner development believe that once we die, we are shown the effects our actions have had on others. With assistance from a higher guidance, we will be able to look at how we can learn the necessary lessons, and be given the opportunity to do so in another life. Then, hopefully, we can act differently and reach a higher note. What is termed 'Divine Justice' does exist in this manner, and it is far more accurate than any earthly justice could ever be. The only one who can 'clear' what is termed your 'bad karma' is you, and you do this via your actions, your motivations with regard to these, and through your learning processes that may be intertwined with others. It is impossible for anyone else to do this for you, just as it is impossible for anyone else to live your life for you.

There is also the notion that individuals who have reached full enlightenment, and what is termed 'freedom of the wheel of karma', return voluntarily to help others. In my personal view, this must represent a big sacrifice since none of us can exist on this Earth without creating karma, be this positive or otherwise. It may also be a little unpleasant for someone who carries such a high vibration to have to spend time around those who are on a considerably lower level. One can only have the deepest respect and gratitude for such amazing individuals.

As far as healers are concerned, it is of the utmost importance to realise that when you have become skilled in energy work, your emanations become much more powerful. If you have issues with people and you think angry thoughts about them for a while, this can affect them in quite a negative fashion, especially if they do not have any energy awareness. Therefore, it is vital to take time to deal with your personal issues, without projecting them onto anyone else. Positive thoughts and feelings towards others are fine, provided you are not attempting to manipulate anyone into doing something for you. Knowledge brings responsibility, and deliberate misuse of it may well cause considerable detours on this wonderful path, including karmic issues that must eventually be balanced.

When it comes to self-healing, you can, of course, make your own choices about how fast you wish to move forward, as long as you take responsibility for what then emerges in your life, and do not blame others for your issues. In the New Age movement, there is much talk about 'coming from the heart', and this is indeed something to aspire to. If you have mastered most of the life lessons related to the chakra system, you may well be able to come from the heart, even in the direst of situations. Whenever you falter in this, however, take another look at how you could respond with a different approach, and also strive to understand the actual lesson you are presented with. It is definitely a requirement on the path of inner development to understand the true meaning of the word forgiveness, which is a quality pertaining to the heart chakra and to letting go.

It can be very tricky putting this into practice, and not merely intellectualising the theoretical concepts, when you consider that many people on this Earth still deliberately harm others for various reasons. Like all of us, such people are subject to the laws of cause and effect, although this is not always immediately apparent. There are also many who feel that the world is unfair and lacking in justice, and that the saying, 'what goes around comes around' is not really valid. Sometimes, one cannot help but be angry, hurt or even traumatised, even when aware of the worlds of energy. It may, therefore, be helpful to realise that when someone has harmed you on purpose, his or her vibration cannot possibly be of a very high note. When you keep thinking about this person, with anger, hurt or similar thoughts and feelings, you will begin to match the low vibration and actually empower the perpetrator who thrives on such energies. This will make it very difficult for you to move beyond the situation.

The best way to deal with such issues, therefore, is to let go completely. Release yourself from this person energetically, and realise that you are on different wavelengths, even if this may prove to be difficult. You do not have to like him/her or be friends. We all have our lessons to learn, but we do not need to accept any form of abusive treatment. When you have let go, and are able to perceive the whole issue in a more detached manner, you (as a healer) can then look carefully at why this event happened in your life. The longer we walk this path, the more we realise that we are not just responsible for much of what happens to us, but also that we have the tools to deal with much that comes our way. This is, of course, not something healers should point out to their clients. For your own development, there is an exercise in chapter seventeen, (Releasing Negativity with Others), that can begin to help with this.

There is the belief in some development circles that souls make contracts to help each other learn lessons, and that sometimes this can result in one person harming another, yet because it was a soul contract, there is no 'karma' involved. I personally find this to be a precarious viewpoint as it implies that hugely damaging behaviour may be fully justifiable on the energy planes. All of us have soul contracts, but we cannot possibly use this notion as an excuse for abusive actions. If you try to do the best you can for yourself, others and the whole, you cannot go too far astray.

One of the warnings that most of us ignore, when we start out on this path, is not to compare ourselves with others. Every single person proceeds in their own way, and it does not matter if someone is in front of you, behind you or walking with you. You may be able to learn from the ones who are a little further ahead; guide those that have not yet come as far and share trials, tribulations as well as joy with those who stand beside you. The further you travel on this path towards ever greater Light, the more care you will take with your thoughts, feelings and actions. Ultimately, this will lead to more and more freedom, and you will cease being negatively affected by what others think of you. You will also be able to respond more effectively to challenges and take greater responsibility rather than reacting badly to upsets.

Where healing others is concerned, the reason for asking for the highest good for our clients is not just because we cannot perceive the bigger picture, but because we want to avoid making mistakes that can cause problems for another. Working energetically with others, and thereby touching on their deepest issues, is sacred work that requires the utmost respect. We can also be grateful for the opportunity for growth that every single client (or student) brings us since it cannot be stated enough: 'the world is a mirror', and on an individual level, all act as mirrors to each other.

16

Self-Healing

Self-healing is an important part of inner development, which is why a healer must be able to self-evaluate. One of the many ways to do this is to become aware of habitual thoughts and emotional processes that hinder rather than promote wholeness. Most such issues are detectable in our subtle anatomy and can be addressed with several self-healing techniques. Although not a substitute for receiving healing from someone else, self-healing is ultimately what all healing is about. Another healer can help and support, but not lead our life for us or learn our lessons. One way to approach the whole topic of self-healing is through the concept of patterns.

Personal Patterns

Everything that exists is part of a pattern. We are surrounded by patterns, carry patterns within us and are also a component of an immense pattern. We incessantly create patterns and are affected by other people's patterns. There is virtually nothing on this Earth that is not part of a pattern or does not have patterns within it. All these patterns are, or ideally should be, in constant motion. Thought and emotional patterns, patterns of behaviour, habitual patterns, disease patterns, family patterns, ancestral patterns, belief patterns and childhood patterns are only a tiny part of this. In addition to patterns, there are cycles, which are repetitive patterns. The ebb and flow of tides, the seasons, night and day, life and death, and so on are familiar patterns that are all predictable to a certain extent. I am well aware of the overuse of the word patterns in this paragraph, but hope it helps to labour the point!

Whenever you give or receive healing energies, you are changing a pattern, hopefully to a slightly higher or at least more balanced note! Everything you think, feel, say or do will affect one or more patterns within or around you, as well as everyone else and the collective. This can be positive or negative, and can be viewed as highly empowering because it demonstrates that we continually create and influence everything and everyone. How you do this is up to you, although the circumstances you find yourself in also play a part. Thoughts and strong feelings are highly instrumental in what we create in our lives, and to become aware of these is the first step to take.

Thought Patterns

Most of us are not consciously aware of the thoughts we think all day, and repetitive thoughts, as well as strong repetitive emotions, register in our subconscious mind and are stored there. They often come to the fore when we have to respond to a situation, and it is sometimes difficult to change habits because of this. It follows that continual positive thinking is the aim, although to accomplish this is not all that easy nor effective if done forcefully, as it may result in repressing negativity rather than dealing with it. By the same token, thinking positively about something for an hour and then reverting to negative self-talk for the rest of the day will not instigate change. The most effective way to deal with the subject of thought is to become aware of what you think about most of the time, and determine your more unhelpful repetitive thought processes. Once you are aware of your most negative thoughts, you can change these by instantly focussing on something else the moment they arise. This could be a favourite flower, crystal, colour or another preferred item. Then, after a second or two, deliberately think about something positive, which could be a favourite holiday or the (positive) outcome of one of your plans. After a while, the flower, crystal or colour will come to mind whenever that negative thought makes itself known, and if you keep at this, it will eventually give up the ghost.

Once you have managed to weed out most of you unhelpful and unnecessary thought processes and replaced them with something useful and beneficial, you are well on the road towards creating a better way forward. Like everything else, this does take time and effort, and it is therefore advisable to tackle just one thing (or rather thought) at a time. You are in a process of change, and slow and steady is always preferable to instigating dramatic shifts. You, and you alone, are in charge of your thought processes, and you have been given the ability to think as a tool to help create and shape your life on Earth.

Delving much deeper into the subject of thought, the inevitable question of 'who is doing the thinking' will come up. Where is this 'you' who is thinking? Is it in your head, in your body or somewhere else? The more you reflect upon this, the more you will begin to know and experience a 'you' that, although still linked to your mind, body and emotions, is in fact outside of these in what can be described as a vast inner world. Such awareness then allows you to start sensing, first fleetingly, and then more strongly, impressions of your Higher Self or your Soul aspect, which is the real You (the capital letter Y indicates from now on that we mean the Higher Self or the Soul by the word, You). The truth is that we are eternal beings who have clothed ourselves in a physical body with the capacity to think, feel and act; in order to experience a certain amount of time on this plane of existence. This concept is, however, only of meaning, when you can relate to it in both theory and practice.

Looking once again at our patterns of thought, much of our behaviour, including the way we think, has been formed in childhood by the influence of our parents and other authority figures. If this has been of a beneficial nature, changing things will not represent too much of a problem, but if not, it may be a little more challenging.

Deep-seated thought patterns are often built up over generations and can be viewed as ancestral patterns. Equally, strong impressions and experiences in early childhood can influence us throughout our lives and be difficult to modify. Much of this often becomes ingrained before the age of seven, which is why many of us do not consciously remember it. There are also cultural patterns of behaviour, political systems, class systems, and so on. The majority of people live and conform according to patterns that their society has set, and those who veer away from these are often considered eccentric or rebels. Most healers will probably recognize this particular trait!

All such influences and experiences are stored in our subconscious and have become part of us, although we rarely recognize this. Another factor relating to the subconscious mind is that it will attract situations in your life according to how you have programmed it. It is well known in development circles that your outer world is mostly a reflection of your inner world, which is why awareness of our thought processes and our subconscious mind is so important. You can liken your subconscious mind to a computer with a huge database. There are several techniques you can use to alter things in your subconscious mind, but if traumatic issues come up, you may need to seek help. There is a subconscious mind meditation in chapter seventeen.

If you wish to let go of redundant patterns and instigate important changes in your life, you can work actively with both your subconscious mind and Higher Self, which has a greater overview of your life plan and purpose. As stated before, this is a huge subject, and mainly outside the scope of this book.

Emotional patterns

Our emotions are also highly instrumental in what we manifest. They are of a slightly slower vibration than our thoughts and give them substance. Like the ability to think, the ability to feel emotion is a tool we use to manifest much of our lives. It is therefore equally important to be aware of what you feel as well as what you think. Repressing or ignoring your feelings is not helpful since these will then grow in strength and overwhelm you when you least expect it.

The main difference between emotion and thought is that emotions flow through us like waves, whereas thoughts are more persistent. There are many examples that illustrate how much our thought and emotional processes affect our lives. If, for instance, you wish to manifest something, have thought about it carefully and are enthusiastic, passionate and optimistic about your plans, you may well get somewhere provided you also take appropriate action. Persistent feelings of insecurity, doubt or other negative emotions, however, will in most cases prevent a favourable outcome.

Another example relating to this subject, is that thoughts and feelings from a group of people can affect us hugely if we are unaware. One can see this, unfortunately more often than not when looking at office politics. Stress has become a big problem in many companies, and this is not just due to massive workloads. Thoughts about not being as proficient as one's colleagues, or feeling unable to finish a project quickly enough, are usually accompanied by worry and anxiety. If there are a considerable number of workers who think and feel the same way, these negative energies become grossly amplified and the atmosphere highly unpleasant. Such stresses also affect one's health and it is for that reason that so many absences due to stress are reported in the business world.

We also know, from experience and the news, how dangerous a large group of people can become when negatively enticed. The destructive emotions amplify, eventually becoming out of control, affecting everyone and then a scenario that is known as mob behaviour takes over. Experienced public speakers often use such know-how to electrify their audience by deliberately using words that strongly provoke feelings. If you look at history, you can see this clearly regarding both beneficial and detrimental outcomes. Equally, if a group of people enjoy themselves, maybe at a festival or concert, the atmosphere can become exhilarating, and afterwards most people feel energized and happy.

Being aware that the ability to feel, like the ability to think, is nothing but a tool you have been given to be able to live in this world, does not mean that you have to consciously change your feelings since this is not possible.

Feelings are often a pointer to what is going on within us and can teach us much about ourselves; they can also be difficult to cope with. When it comes to using energy work to help with these, the Bach Flower Essences, as mentioned earlier, can be invaluable in helping to address emotional issues since they represent the positive alternative to negative emotional states. They flood the emotional layer of the energy field with the relevant positive quality, such as a feeling of get up and go, if one has the Monday morning feeling too often, or a sense of being more focussed when suffering from a grasshopper mentality. In the first example the essence Hornbeam is indicated and in the second one, the essence Wild Oat.

If you have challenging emotional issues, the following technique is very effective in getting these out of your system. Take some time to yourself and begin to write all your feelings on a piece of paper. You may find that more and more negative issues emerge, but keep writing until there is nothing left. Then make the conscious decision to let go of it all, either by shredding the paper or burning the lot safely and responsibly and disposing of the ashes with care. After this, link to the Light and ask for healing energies to help replace that which you have let go of. You may be surprised how much has left you and how much lighter you feel.

As you progress in your personal development, you will able to experience the real You for longer periods of time, and then if you become upset for some reason in your day-to-day life, you will start to engage less and be able to observe your feelings more. The negative feelings will then lessen in intensity because you are becoming fully aware of what is truly going on. This is not about functioning like a robot, but about realising more and more who you are on the most profound levels. Positive emotions such as love, joy and harmony will still be actively experienced!

The following chapter includes a few basic self-healing techniques. If difficult issues come up, or if you feel you are out of your depth while doing these exercises, please seek advice from a healer, counsellor or similar therapist. Forgive me for repeating this a few times, but it is important. The exercises are also not meant to be used on others and please only try out what you feel completely comfortable with.

17

Self-Healing Methods

Ultimately all healing is about supporting and also empowering, which is why no healers worth their salt will make their clients dependent on them. Most make their clients aware of simple self-help methods such as grounding, clearing and strengthening their energy field, which anyone can do with ease. If a client is open to it, a healer may also point him/her in the direction of certain books or anything else appropriate that can be of help. Healers, however, also need to take care of themselves which is why a few more intricate methods are included in this chapter.

Subconscious Mind Meditation

This meditation is for when you wish to change or create something in your life. Before you start, ensure your intent is clear and that you will not be disturbed. Then sit in a comfortable chair and ensure you are fully relaxed. You could also hold a favourite crystal to help you stay grounded and alert. The meditation is as follows:

Ground, centre and link to the Light and take yourself to your favourite landscape. As you walk along a path, you see a small building and when you enter it there is a staircase going down as well as an elevator. If you take the elevator, press the button 'subconscious mind' and when you land there and you exit, you will see a big golden door. If you prefer to walk down the stairs, you will see this door when you arrive at the bottom. Then imagine that the door opens, enter and find yourself in a huge square room. The wall facing you consists of a large screen in front of which is a table with a keyboard and a chair in which you now take a seat. There are also a few buttons you can press on the side of the table. Next to one of these you see the word 'ceiling'. You look up and you can see the ceiling which is very high and part of it looks like it can open up.

Focus now on the screen and know that you can project your intent on to it. You can picture the situation you wish to find yourself in and also type what you wish for on the keyboard and see it appear at the bottom or top of your picture. Some people prefer to just write the words, others only picture what they want to experience and some do both. Once you are happy with it all, you press the ceiling button and part of it will slide to the side and a beautiful golden light fills the room and illuminates the picture. This is the Light from your Higher Self. Look for a moment at the picture and focus on how it would feel when your wish has become a reality. You can now press the Enter button and once the screen has cleared, press the ceiling button again, which then allows the room to revert to normal.

After this exit the room, close the door and walk back up the stairs or take the elevator and press the button 'conscious awareness'. Leave the building and walk back through the landscape into your room and then ground yourself.

You can personalise this meditation as you wish, since this room represents your subconscious mind. Remember to only picture positive scenarios and to keep any wording in the present tense. Also ensure that what you wish for is something you really want and that you also believe that it is achievable. You can also get creative and use the keyboard to delete unhelpful programming etc. but in that case always replace what you delete with a positive alternative.

This meditation helped me stop smoking many years ago. I decided to be brutal and programmed my subconscious mind to make me feel physically sick whenever I inhaled cigarette smoke and from that moment stopped smoking. It was not a pleasant way to go about this but highly effective. A few years ago, I did try to take a puff and immediately felt sick! After more than thirty-five odd years, my subconscious mind remembered what I had asked it to do and carried out the instruction.

Affirmation Technique

Affirmations are short, positive sentences that you repeat frequently in order to help create something. It is another means of introducing what you wish into your subconscious mind, which will then endeavour to carry this out. You must always keep the sentences in the present. If, for instance, you weigh eighty kilos and wish to lose ten of these, your affirmation must not state: 'I am losing ten kilos' or 'I am in the process of losing weight' because this will not be effective. Instead your affirmation should be: 'My weight is seventy kilos' and then repeat this often, especially before going to sleep. You need, of course, to help this process along by altering your diet or lifestyle accordingly.

When you are repeating your affirmation, you could perceive yourself as already having what it is you wish and also being grateful for it! You could also visualise the affirmation in colour and project it into your subconscious mind. If you are forgetful, you could draw your affirmation on a piece of paper and hang it on your wall where you can see it often, so you are reminded of it. You could either write the words or draw a picture, depending on what works best for you. You can also tune a crystal with your affirmation and carry it with you. As with all healing and development work, only create and use affirmations once you are very sure about what it is you wish to change or acquire. We often wish for something and when we receive it do not want it any longer. It is best to avoid this since it may hinder rather than help you.

Vowel Sounds and Mantras

An exercise to help energize or balance your chakra system is to chant vowel sounds. The way to do this is to imagine the sound on the in-breath and then let the sound out on the out-breath. You can also imagine and direct the overriding colour vibration of the relevant chakra into it on the in-breath. Take around three to five such breaths for each chakra, and at the end ground yourself and draw in your energy field. The sounds for both the base and the sacral are OOO (like you), for the solar plexus it is OH (like more), for the heart the sound is AH (like star) for the throat it is EH (like well), for the brow it is EEE (like see) and for the crown it is MMM (a closed sound). Different people use different sounds and this does not really matter; just use what works for you, and be thoughtful of neighbours who may be put off by the 'noise'.

Mantras are phrases that have been thought, voiced and chanted over thousands of years. Most come from the East and the one mostly used in the West is the 'I am that I am'. It is important to know exactly what a mantra represents before you use it, because they are incredibly powerful and you are linking to mighty energies that have been and are being expressed by millions of people for thousands of years. I had a very interesting experience on a course where we ended a day by chanting the OM, which is an Eastern mantra that represents the Word of creation and is extremely powerful.

The sound was flat to say the least, so I suggested we try the AMEN which means 'so be it', although going further back it comes from AMON RA, both of which are considered the same as the OM, but relating to the Western tradition. When we tried to do it this way, the energy in the room completely changed and the group sounded like an experienced choir having a fantastic time. The chant also produced beautiful overtones and I always wondered if doing it the other way around, with a group of people from the Far East, would have a similar outcome, but have not yet had the chance to try this out.

Releasing Negativity with Others

This is a powerful technique which you must do from start to finish. Make sure, therefore, that you are sitting in a position where you cannot possibly fall asleep, and link to the Light and your guidance. The intent is that your wish to clear and heal redundant and unhelpful patterns between yourself and another person (always add that what you do is for the highest good). Visualize yourself in a landscape of your choice, create a golden circle of Light on the ground and step into this. The circle is big enough to be comfortable in. You then create an identical circle facing you, a few metres away, and invite the person in question into this circle. You can say to him or her that you wish to clear any negative issues between you and then may become aware of debris starting to form in the space between you.

There may even be a few links connecting you, such as ropes or similar substances. If this happens, take an imaginary knife or other suitable tool, cut them out of your energy field and cover the relevant areas with blue or gold Light. Place all that you have cut away outside of your circle, together with the other debris. Once this process is finished, wave goodbye to the other person and see him/her recede back into Light. You may then be left with much debris. You can gather this together and either set it alight or bury it. Just notice that when you set it alight, a positive (to you) symbol may emerge from the flames, such as one or more stars or butterflies. If you have buried the debris become aware that there are flowers growing on top of the earth. Once all is done, you let the circles fade away, leave your landscape and come back into your normal state of awareness and ground yourself.

Please note that what you are doing is beneficial. You are, in fact, clearing away your own negativity towards the other person as well as their negativity (pertaining to you personally) being emitted towards you. You are not obliged to take on board negativity from others, and you are always allowed to address and clear any form of negativity that is yours. This technique can be helpful in maintaining relationships or moving on in a positive manner. It is not advisable to do this with your own children before they have reached the age of puberty, but with regard to teenagers and those who are older, it can much improve relationships.

Releasing Ancestral Patterns

Although your ancestors are not necessarily members of your Soul group, you have incarnated in to your bloodline for certain reasons. Even if your ancestors were not the most loving, law- abiding or respectable folk, they will have contributed to who you are, with regard to your personality, on this plane of existence. Many of your good as well as more regrettable qualities, have provided and are providing you with the opportunity to fulfil your purpose in this, your present incarnation. You therefore have reason to be thankful, even if you wish to change certain undesirable traits or qualities.

Many of us Light workers have chosen to incarnate in a specific bloodline, in order to stop a 'trend' of behaviour, thereby giving descendants the possibility of a different way forward. Ancestral healing means changing necessary issues. You cannot heal your ancestors; you can, however, help heal undesirable effects they may have caused. You can also offer Light and Love, as well as forgiveness if this is appropriate. This may well help transmute lower energies into a slightly higher note! You can also release traits within yourself that do not serve you any longer and the following meditation is one way of doing this.

Ancestral Issues Release Exercise

First of all, make sure you know exactly what it is you wish to release and change. This could be a pattern of illness that has repeated itself over generations, certain patterns of behaviour or anything else that you do not wish to perpetuate. Once you have established this, go into healing mode, enter a meditative state and reflect on the many ancestors who have contributed to the specific trait you now wish to release. You may perceive them as a row of people, whose faces you cannot see clearly. Stand in front of them, say who you are, and thank them for all the traits they have passed on to you throughout the ages. You can say that you are deeply grateful, but the world has changed, and you wish now to release a few of those built-in characteristics, since they do not serve you any longer. Ask the Angelic and the Light that you may be a channel for the quality of love and gratitude and channel this towards all of your ancestors. Then let the picture fade and proceed with your own healing. Ask for the healing energies to help clear what is appropriate and also infuse you with the new, so you can start to take this on board.

You can adapt and extend this meditation as you feel comfortable. The reason meditations in the book are kept as short as possible is so you can remember them.

Self-Healing with Flowers

If you are out of sorts, buy a bunch of flowers, tune them for your healing process and place them in the room you find yourself most in. You may well be surprised at the outcome. Sometimes the flowers wilt after just one or two days or even in a matter of hours. This means they have either finished with their job, or that you may need additional help. At other times, they stay fresh for up to a month, which is way beyond the norm, and can mean they are working very hard indeed to help you. There are those who believe flowers should not be picked and should be allowed to live out their natural time in nature. I personally feel that tuning cut flowers for the purpose of healing gives them more meaning. When you tune flowers for your self-healing process, do not forget to also express your gratitude! You can make use of this simple method for anyone. If you know a friend is going through a rough patch, you can give them a bunch of flowers that you have tuned for their highest good and well-being.

Stress Release Method

If you are affected by stress, it is important to relax both your body and your mind at least once a day. This does not need to take more than ten or fifteen minutes. Make sure you will not be disturbed and sit or lie down. Take a few deep breaths, and imagine that you are sitting or lying down beneath a favourite tree in a peaceful landscape. Link to the Light and ask that you may receive the healing that you need. Then focus your attention on your feet, and gently breathe a pale blue, green or golden colour into them. Then let the healing energies touch your feet. If you are given different colours, focus on those. Two or three breaths for each body part is sufficient. After your feet, address your legs, lower back, the whole of your back, stomach area, chest, throat, back of neck, shoulders, arms and hands, the back of your head and your face, finishing with your jaw muscles. You could play relaxing music whilst you are doing this, or hold a crystal. Orbicular Jasper is particularly appropriate for this. Afterwards thank the Light and ground yourself. It is very effective to do this just before you go to sleep!

Opening and Closing Chakras

When giving or receiving healing energies, meditating or focusing on the worlds of energy, one's energy field expands and the seven main chakras spin faster than usual. This is often called the opening of chakras. At the end of such work it is necessary to draw in one's energy field and slow the spin of the chakras back to a state of ordinary awareness, sometimes called 'closing' chakras, although a more accurate terminology is 'slowing down' chakras.

More often than not, this happens naturally during the grounding process, but at times it is prudent to also ensure that your chakra system is back to its usual state. The way to do this for yourself is via thought, using imagery. You can imagine that each chakra represents a door that gently closes; you can imagine that each chakra is covered with a veil; you can imagine that each chakra is a flower that changes into a bud or that each chakra glows as a bright light that you dim a little. You can use any other imagery that you feel is appropriate. The intent is to slow the spin of the chakras to their ordinary day-to-day state.

When doing this for a client at the end of a healing session (having let go of your link to the Light and healing energies), you focus your intent on the slowing down of the chakras and then do this simultaneously for your client and yourself, chakra by chakra, from the crown to the base. After that you ground yourself and your client.

If you feel the need to create a strong protection over each of your chakras, you can visualize each chakra as an open flower that shrinks to a bud and then to a small point of light. You then place an equal-armed cross over that point of light.

18

Healing Others

As indicated in an earlier chapter, when you start to practise professionally, you will often attract clients who have issues that you have had in the past. The reason for this is that those who come to you, usually have a similar vibration to yours. After a while, you may notice that most of your new clients have different issues. This means that you have changed something within yourself and can therefore be helpful to more people. It can also happen that you get a client whom you find difficult, and usually this means that s/he is has come to you not just for help, but also to show you something highly relevant.

On rare occasions someone may come to you who you feel you cannot help. This usually becomes apparent once you start the session. You could sense that the energies that you channel are being returned to you which is a highly unpleasant sensation. When this happens, you must stop the session, say that the energies that you are channelling seem not to be right, and that it is best you refer him/her to another healer. Always take the responsibility for this upon yourself and do not charge your client for your time. In my thirty odd years of healing this has only happened to me twice. One person did not really want healing but was coerced by a friend to try it out, and was very relieved when I stopped the session. The other person needed a different type of help, which I found out when we discussed the situation. In both cases it would have been counterproductive had I continued with the session.

If you are personally concerned about certain diseases or symptoms, do not treat clients who suffer from these. Your worry will come across and you could also risk taking on board such issues. Usually when someone makes an appointment, s/he will mention any severe problems and you can then refer her/him to a colleague if you feel uncomfortable. Always make sure that clients do not become overly dependent on you. Healing is about empowering others and usually a few sessions are more than enough. Often clients come back for regular 'top up' sessions and that is fine, but if someone keeps coming for no good reason, it is important to stop this. As mentioned earlier, you could make them aware of self-help books, basic exercises or point them in the direction of a workshop or short course that is relevant to them.

Always explain to your clients that at times present issues may intensify a little before they improve and make sure that they have the opportunity to contact you should this happen in case they need reassurance. Healers call this a healing crisis which can manifest up to three days after a session. It can also happen during a session, in which case you must take appropriate action, which is covered in healer training. Admin issues, code of conduct, health and safety, how to run a practice, listening skills and many other more practical topics are taught on all healing courses and are therefore not included in this book.

Although how to do healing is covered throughout the book, I will include a basic description of how it is usually done. Before a client comes, ground, centre and link to the Light and the Angelic (but not to the client). Once the client is with you and made comfortable, you then also link energetically to the client and take him/her through a brief relaxation. Then ask that you may be a channel for healing for your client and once the energies are flowing through you, re-link to your client and quietly ask their Higher Self for permission (as a sign of respect). When this is given, you start by placing your hand very briefly over the crown chakra and then move through the whole system and only linger where this is needed. Once you reach the base chakra, you can check if any of the others need more work. When this is done, connect the energies of the chakra system at the back, by placing one hand at the very top of the spine and the other at the bottom of the spine. If the client is lying down you channel this from the side. After that you address various layers of the energy field that may need it. You can also check if any of the horizontal gridlines need to be addressed and then always finish with the central vertical line which anchors this system. You then clear the energy field and when finished, ground the client.

The reason you do not link to a client before they are with you is that this can unground them and there is also no point since our energy field is in constant motion and you are only supposed to address what is needed when you start your healing work. You must be linked to the Light before the client is with you because the initial chat and the relaxation process form part of the session.

Distant Healing

Healing can be facilitated distantly for the simple reason that everything and everyone is interconnected. If you think about someone, you connect with that person energetically because thought is energy. It is also instantaneous. Healing energy is more intense than ordinary thought since it is of a much higher note, and when crystals are used the energies become even more defined. There are, however, some who emit healing energies to others without asking their permission, which is something that can be viewed as highly questionable.

If you are a healer, and wish to channel healing to someone, why not contact them and ask? If they know you and have not asked you, they probably do not want it. If they are not in a position to ask you, you could always pray for them. Prayer does not involve the channelling of energies and is perfectly OK to do for anyone. Equally, it is possible that someone has already asked another healer for help. There could also be a very good reason for someone not wanting healing from you or anyone else.

It can be an unpleasant experience to have unasked for healing projected onto you, especially if the healer in question does not have a very clear channel or s/he is not on the same wavelength or energetic vibration as you are. If crystals are used, it can be difficult to keep these powerful energies at bay, and it is also possible that there is a lack of experience on the healer's part. It can also happen that a person who is receiving unwanted healing energies will become ungrounded, and if driving a car or in similar circumstances, this can be very dangerous. We are responsible for our actions, and there is no reason for giving healing to those who have not asked for it.

Virtually all techniques can be used distantly, and when you focus on a client, always perceive him or her as healthy (even if this is not the case), whilst you are facilitating the session. Also ensure you use clean crystals and do not forget to clear them again after the session has finished. Some healers use a photograph of a client in order to achieve a better focus and that is fine. Just put it away carefully after you have finished with it, or return it to the client. It is also necessary to agree on a time so that your client can relax and to ask for feedback the day after, so you can ensure all has gone well. The best time to facilitate a distant healing session is in the evening before your client goes to sleep.

A distant healing session is energetically more focussed than a hands-on session, because there is no human interaction such as receiving someone, chatting a little and so forth. It is a direct and immediate transmission of healing energies. Like all healing work, it is important to carefully record what occurred, which tools (if any) you used and why, and also note down feedback from your client or any advice you may have given.

At times, when there are places where many people suffer, such as in war or disaster zones, you can offer distant healing. In this case your intent must be to offer the energies that you channel to those who ask for it. Most people in dire need will think, say or even scream something like 'God help me' and that is equivalent to asking. Since in such circumstances there are so many people in need, you are not interfering with anyone against their will.

19

Planetary Healing

Planetary healing has become increasingly, necessary mainly because of the damaging actions of many human beings. The biggest issue is the toxicity we have created and still are creating in the elements of earth, water, air and also the space around us. Plastic, pesticides, the destruction of major forests, radiation and toxic emanations of much of our technology are only a few examples of this. We are part of nature and without it we cannot possibly survive, so in a sense we are destroying ourselves. By facilitating healing for nature and the planet, we emit an energy that, apart from being beneficial to the Earth itself, also addresses the cause of the destruction. There are quite a number of healers who alone or in groups facilitate planetary healing and one can begin to see the effect this has.

More and more individuals are already instigating change by cleaning up beaches and other places from plastic and other debris. There are also quite a few who have been planting countless trees and helping bees to survive to just name a few other actions. Many young people are starting to protest seriously and rightly demand we treat our Earth better and politicians and big corporations will soon have no other option but to listen and act. Without wanting to diminish the incredible efforts of all those individuals, I believe that healing and Light energies are impressing all those who are open to such higher vibrations to act accordingly.

There is no need to use complicated techniques in order to facilitate planetary healing. Linking to the Light and the Angelic, and asking to be a channel for the benefit and healing of nature, is very effective. You could connect to plant or tree energies, ask if help is needed and then channel accordingly. There are unfortunately individuals who misuse living herb and plant energies for questionable magical practices and you could help free these. The way to do this is to link to the Light and (Arch) Angel energies, and then have the intent to free such unfortunate bound nature spirits. You then channel the energies in general and ask that these beings are released from their bond and returned to the guardianship of the Angelic, so they can continue with their true purpose, which is for the health and well-being of nature. The reason it is advisable to link to such mighty Angelic energies is that sometimes, such issues can be a little dark and you will be safe if doing it in this way. If you feel uncomfortable about such work, leave it aside.

Sometimes a healer who does not channel energies for a while may starts to feel a little awkward. They can be feeling over energized, scattered, restless or experience similar states of being. When this happens, go into your garden or a park and quietly channel light and healing for the benefit of nature. This will also help balance your own energies. You could include the various elements in such work.

If you are interested in helping to clear dark and stagnant energies in the world, it is important that you do not have an overly emotional connection to what you are focussing on. One example to illustrate this is the issue of the concentration camps of the Second World War. One healer I know feels quite deeply about this, and was part of a group that did an Earth healing in order to help transmute some of the horrendous energies that are still embedded in such places. This person felt ill for quite some time afterwards, and the reason for this is that by channelling energies to a place, you are linking to it. If you are detached that is fine, but if you have intense feelings about it, you risk taking on board some of the more difficult emanations. I also had the impression that the healer in question had a memory of the camps from another lifetime and this may have brought up subconscious issues. As mentioned in the section on strengthening your energy field, you cannot always keep energies out if you strongly relate to these. In many such dark places, the fabric of the earth and surroundings are so much imbued with the energies of hate, fear, pain and so forth, that it may take years to help clear and transmute these. Many spots in our world have a long history of negativity and there are healers who do nothing else but try to clear and transmute this. There is no doubt that their work is helpful to all.

Subtle Planes

Healers also need to be aware of the many subtle levels that surround us collectively. This knowledge is useful with regard to both planetary healing and inner development. All levels can be experienced in profound meditation.

The **etheric layer** around the planet is the domain of the Devic kingdom which consists of all the energies behind the whole of nature. As with us, this layer demonstrates the health and vitality of the earthly plane. If you are interested in working closely with nature spirits, this is the plane where you can find them.

When you find yourself in nature, link to it by focussing on the trees, plants and flowers that surround you. Then be still, and become aware of the subtle energies that are always willing to communicate. Channelling Light to nature itself is always appreciated and you can ask the Angelic, which is in overall charge of it, to distribute the energies where they are needed most. If you channel for the elements, it is advised not to leave any out, because they are strongly interlinked and all of them need it!

The **astral layer** comes next and this is a vast domain both of incredible beauty but also the opposite. It is the plane of dreams (and nightmares), unicorns, dragons and similar species which are written about in fairy tales. It is also a place where many of those who leave this world initially go, as well as where those who cannot move forward reside. Within this astral world there are numerous levels, both of light and shadow and it is advised to be careful when going there deliberately. Shamanic people from all cultures are highly familiar with the astral worlds and travel there often.

This layer is also a place where you may have to face your worst fears, especially if you are on the path of inner development and have reached certain levels. It can be a place of magic and similar practices as well. On festivals such as Halloween, the veil between the astral world and ours is thin, which is why so many people celebrate this. It can also be a plane of illusion and glamour and the seat of all potent emotional energies that we are emitting and have emitted. There are 'clouds' of both positive and negative emotions, and when we feel strongly, we can attract similar feelings towards us from the astral worlds as well as add to these forms. Everyone visits this place in their sleep and we often meet others there although this is rarely remembered. If you strongly think of a place you wish to visit before you fall asleep, it is highly possible you will do so and dream about it!

The **lower mental layer** is the plane where all thought forms both from conscious and subconscious minds are lodged, especially those that are intense. This is also not always an easy layer to spend much time in, since much of it not of as high a vibration as one would wish (to put it mildly). This layer, as the two previous ones, affects us quite strongly. The best way to make a difference here is to become aware of your thought processes and then work through the more undesirable ones in order to reach a higher note. We cannot destroy energy but we can transmute it, and the best and most effective way to start to do this is with regard to our personal energies. This mental plane is easily perceived in most big offices or other places of work. All of these, over time, acquire an identity, which is more constant than the level of emotions. If this identity is not as one would wish, it is at present extremely difficult to change, mostly due to a lack of knowledge. Hopefully in the future, this subject will become better understood and then those in charge, provided they are interested in a better office climate, will be able to make a huge difference.

The **higher mental layer** is where everything becomes much lighter and of a higher vibration. It is a place of beauty and inspiration and many artists find their creativity there. It is also the place where the Angelic is more easily reached and where you can communicate with various forms of guidance. If you need a break from it all, this is the place to go to in meditation! Currently not many human beings are acutely aware of this plane of existence. One of the reasons for this can be the hurry everyone seems to be in nowadays. Although every single human being has an aspect of beauty within them, many are only aware of their physical vehicle and often try to change this using plastic surgery, not always with positive results.

Real beauty is a thing of the soul; it inspires and uplifts, is elegant and harmonious and transcends the mundane. You can sometimes see this beauty in the eyes and face of a child or a very old person, you can see it in nature, in flowers, sunsets and land or seascapes. You can also find it in paintings and beautiful music or dance, and the words grace, refinement and loveliness are other words that describe the quality of beauty. They say that once upon a time the Angels walked the Earth, and this must have been when the higher mental layer was prominent. I fervently hope that such an age will come again!

The **causal layer** contains the blueprint of our world and it is vast. Everything that has happened, is happening and will happen is contained there. This concept is not easy to understand because it transcends time and space. Once could perceive it as a huge library where information can be accessed, but not all of it is open to us for obvious reasons. This library is also called the 'Akashic Records'. If you are able to reach this level, you will meet guardians who are there to make sure that you only receive the knowledge you are supposed to, and which is in line with your place and purpose in the world. If you want to visit this place, ask beforehand that you are only guided to what is of immediate relevance to you, otherwise you may get lost!

The world of archetypes, mythologies and all the eternal wisdom also forms part of this level and so does our history, including that of other civilizations that inhabited this planet before ours. There is both Light and darkness there, truth and distortion with regard to virtually anything you can think of and also the story of all of your (and everyone else's) incarnations.

The **spiritual layer** is where all the beliefs and ideals in their purest form are to be found. It is a place of high wisdom, and also where guidance of a high, if not highest note makes its presence known. Distortions with regard to various beliefs and ideals are also stored here and therefore it is not always an easy level to find oneself in. Discernment is one of the many important qualities for a Light worker to develop, especially if s/he is interested in accessing this level. Spirituality in this context must not be confused with a specific religion. All beliefs and ideals, including those we may never have heard of form part of this level.

The **divine layer** is the one where you find the highest vibrations possible in this world. It is difficult to access or even stay in this plane for longer than a few moments, because it is pure Light. It is also the place where the highest choir of the Angelic has its place, the Seraphim which are beings of pure love. It is stated that the energies of these Angels are so immense that a Human being cannot look upon them. Whenever we call upon such beings of the highest Light, we receive this only to the levels we can cope with since we would burn to a crisp otherwise.

Because our plane of existence is a plane of duality, there are also difficult places on this high level. These are, however, mainly about subtle but no less perilous delusions that can lead eminent initiates off their path. Our world is indeed multi-dimensional and to explore it on more profound levels is definitely worthwhile, provided we do not lose ourselves in these energies and ensure we are always fully grounded and back into an ordinary state of awareness after our energy work!

20

Child, Animal and Group Healing

Children and Healing

There are a few guidelines on healing children, especially if they have not yet reached puberty. When children are small, they are very much affected by the energies of their parents or those who care for them. Babies and toddlers are strongly connected to the energy field of their mothers and if they are unhappy or fretful (provided they are physically well and not in need of medical treatment), it could be the mother who is in need of some assistance, although this is not always the case. It is not easy to come from the world of Light into ours and babies and toddlers sometimes need a little time to adjust to this. The same goes for new parents!

It is not advisable to address chakras of children before the age of puberty and most certainly not to use crystals, including so-called chakra sets on them. The reason for this is that it is not wise to interfere with the process of the initial formation of chakras in children. This could well hinder rather than help them evolve towards their path and purpose in life. You will find guidance on what you can do instead later in this chapter.

To give one example, very young children, even those below the age of seven, now have to do tests in school or pre-school. This is fine if they do well, but if not, it can set up a lifetime of low self-esteem, especially if 'failing the test' is not handled in a caring and appropriate manner. In this scenario, the chakra affected would be the solar plexus, which would be in its first stage of formation. Placing a crystal on it or infusing this centre with energy would not erase this experience and could actually hinder the natural development. Fostering healthy self-esteem in an ordinary fashion is the best possible answer in such a case. I personally believe it is not for nothing that in my youth children did not start school before the age of six or seven and were not expected to do much more than play and enjoy themselves. Unfortunately, nowadays not many people can afford for one parent not to work for a few years, but being encouraging and positively counteracting any such unfortunate experiences is the best way to deal with these scenarios.

If a child needs healing and you are not familiar with this, it is best to refer it to an experienced healer who is accustomed to working with children. If that is not possible, then just channel energy into the energy field of a child, where you can perceive blockages, for a brief moment. Tiny children could sit on their mother's lap and the energies would be channelled towards the mother. With children, always ask the Angelic for help. Each of us has what is called a Guardian Angel and this is very prominent, especially in small children.

Animals and Healing

Animals are highly receptive to energy healing with or without the use of tools such as crystals. This form of healing does bring up certain questions and the considerations are very different from healing human beings. Animals are more strongly connected to the collective or group soul of their species than humans are, since their expression of individuality is less pronounced. It is also worthwhile to look at different groups of animals with regard to healing work. One can divide the animal kingdom into several different types. There are wild animals, wild animals in captivity, farm animals, working animals and pets. There is also a difference between mammals, reptiles, fish, birds and insects.

Healing means to help restore to wholeness, and in case of wild animals in captivity, this can actually have adverse effects. A relatively peaceful wild animal which has become used to being in captivity could change its behaviour when restored energetically to its natural state of well-being. If zoo animals or other wild animals that perform for the public receive healing, they could turn on their keepers or owners if restored to their original nature. This does therefore merit serious contemplation. Equally, the reason that quite a number of animals are not well, is the way we treat their environment. Currently there are huge issues with bees (and butterflies) which some believe are due to technology and pesticides. Without such insects we cannot survive, but healing the bees energetically is not going to help if the cause of their illness is not addressed. It follows that when facilitating distant healing for the bee population, the true intention must be for the relevant humans to find and implement a solution to this problem. Serious reflection is definitely necessary before facilitating such work.

Farm animals are usually fine, provided they are not abused and if so, healing will not help their situation, although it could in certain circumstances ease suffering. Channelling healing and Light to the cause of animal abuse by humans, would come under planetary healing. Fortunately, there are now many people who are actively trying to change some of the appalling conditions in which some animals are kept and we can only hope this will continue.

Things are slightly different with working animals and pets, since these are more closely connected with and used to people. Many pets, especially dogs and cats, strongly relate to their owner's health and well-being as well as their environment and are therefore often out of sorts in relation to this. Provided they are treated well, most such animals are healthy, and if anything is amiss, a visit to the vet or those who practise behavioural therapies for animals will bring back the necessary balance. Energy healing is always complementary to this. Although animals also have a chakra system, this is slightly different from that of Human beings, and addressing their chakras directly may prove to be a little too invasive. What you can do is run your hand over the etheric layer of the animal and you will then pick up anything that is amiss. Then gently clear these places and channel energies in order to replenish what you have cleared. Most animal healers I know work mainly with cats, dogs and horses.

If you are interested in animal healing and do not wish to become a vet, it is important to attend a relevant course where you will learn about animal behaviour, herbs and other practical issues. There are also those who use homeopathy or other essences to treat animals. This is, however, different from crystal and energy healing and boundaries must be kept. When you are asked to facilitate healing for an animal, please make sure the owner has taken the animal to a vet and also adhere to current codes of conduct concerning this.

Group Healing

When a few healers gather together this presents a great opportunity to receive a group healing, which is extremely powerful. To do this, healers first of all place themselves in a circle, link and ask that they may be a channel for healing energies for the person in the centre of the circle. When this person enters the centre, healers just think of his or her name and open themselves up to channel. Usually around four to five minutes is more than enough. It is interesting to note that not all healers will be given energies for each person in the centre – only the most appropriate channels for each 'client' are used.

Many years ago, I was part of a group of healers in a clinic, and we invited all clients prepared to wait after their session the opportunity to also receive a group healing. We had quite a few spectacular (positive) outcomes! When doing this, it is important that one healer leads the group into meditation and also at the end closes the group, making sure everyone is back to an ordinary state of awareness and that the excess energies are dispersed correctly. It is also important to clear the space afterwards.

21

Death and Dying

There is one certainty in life and that is that at some stage we will leave our physical bodies behind for good. It is called dying or death, but as most healers know or believe, this represents only a significant change. Not everyone is of that opinion, so it is necessary to keep your personal beliefs or knowledge to yourself when you are supporting someone during this process and be careful in your communications. When someone is close to death, the Angelic is always present, although those who are in this situation are not always aware of this.

Crystals are rarely used in the case of facilitating healing for someone who is preparing to leave this Earth. Crystals anchor energies which is not required in such a case and it is also not appropriate to address the chakra system other than fleetingly. If the person you are supporting loves crystals, you could give them a few small ones or a slightly bigger crystal to hold. If the person is a crystal healer, he or she will have personal crystals and decide upon this for him/herself.

Healing for those who are in the process of dying is done in a slightly different manner. Bach Flower Essences can be used instead of crystals, provided you are qualified to advise on these. If the client is fearful there are a number of essences that can be of help. Rock Rose is the one for acute states of fear, Aspen for fear of the unknown and Cherry Plum for fear of losing control. There are also instances when people, even when in immense discomfort, cling to life because of the distress of their loved ones. This is because we are so strongly connected on energetic levels. It may be one of the reasons why people so often die when their loved ones are not there. It is, of course, not up to a healer to point this out, but you could ask for help from the Light in such a scenario. If appropriate, something will happen that may give you an opening to give information with regard to helpful flower essences. Red Chestnut is the Bach Flower essence that can help release worry for others and the remedy for grief or shock is Star of Bethlehem.

Flowers are also wonderful healing tools in such a case. A bunch of flowers can be tuned for the client (although this is not always permitted in hospitals) and will emit a peaceful energy. Flowers enable an immediate link to the Angelic and their beauty and energy is always of benefit.

The way to facilitate a healing session for someone who is in the process of dying is to link to the highest levels possible and then ask to be used as a channel for the client as is appropriate. You may find that much energy is flowing through you or that you are just 'holding the space'. If energies are being given, you then mainly channel these towards the client without addressing any of the energy systems. If there is pain, you could gently channel energies into the etheric layer of the energy field just using your hands or a flower, rather than using a crystal.

If only a little energy is given, just sit with the client for a good while, keeping your high link whilst maintaining this serene space. It is more a question of being there than of doing anything and, in a sense, you are acting as a bridge between the two worlds enabling the transition with as much ease as possible. Some may benefit from a guided meditation. If this is the case you must first discuss with the client what they would like. There will be no need to ground the client at the end, especially if they wish to remain in a state of deep peace and relaxation.

When you work with those who are in the process of dying, it is imperative that you receive support for yourself. Never underestimate how such an intense experience can affect you and you may need someone with whom to talk about it or to have healing yourself. Working with death and dying is specialised work and not many healers are drawn to this. If you are one of them, however, know that you are doing incredibly valuable work!

22

Past and Other Lives

Most healers believe as well as know that they have lived many lifetimes and often remember parts of these. We may have been both male and female, of different races, cultures and nationalities. We may have been rich or poor, weak or strong, good or bad and had many different professions. The possibilities are endless. The concept of past lives is more recognized in Eastern countries, although there are also quite a number of people in the West who have had strong personal experiences of past lives. A number of TV programmes have been aired about this subject and there is also a therapy called regression therapy, available for those in need of this.

During a crystal and/or energy healing session it can happen that a client finds him or herself in a so-called past life, experiencing something highly unpleasant. The reason for this is that the healing has triggered a memory from another time. If this happens, you help the client through this experience without influencing what is occurring. If the memory is very painful, you must make your client aware that s/he is experiencing something from another time. Equally that s/he is safe in your presence and observing something that has already happened. You could suggest to clients, when this occurs, that they go through this experience as if they are seeing a movie. Then lead them safely through the experience, and when it is finished, state firmly that they are back with you in your healing room and ask them to relax again. You can then proceed with the session but only to clear, protect and then ground the energy field. After this the client may want to speak about the experience and it is important to allow him/her to do this.

Past life experiences are rarely glamorous and the memory that surfaces is usually something that you need to address or take on board. Those who remember numerous 'past lives' where they were powerful people or those in high authority, and where everything was wonderful, can be trying to escape something difficult in the present life. If your client experiences a memory from a past life and finds this difficult to process, you may need to refer him/her to a regressionist.

To take this a little further, there is also the concept that in a much higher dimension, where there is no time and space, we live all our lives at the same time. The best analogy I have come across regarding this is to view it as a giant puzzle with many pieces. Your present life represents only one of those pieces, and is the main one you are focussing on. This concept also opens up huge possibilities with regard to your own development and self-healing processes. You could emit Light to the whole of the puzzle and carefully note what happens. You can also channel healing Light to your 'past' lives from your perspective as well as your future experiences, either in this, or in other lives. It is very important, however, to carefully reflect on possible consequences and only do this when you are completely sure about it. This information is also not to be shared or practised with clients and only meant for your personal interest.

23

Dealing with Negative Influences

This chapter may be a little difficult for some to read since it can come across as marginally negative. It is, however, essential for healers to understand about various forms of negativity, which is why I have gone into so much detail in the following pages.

Most of the negative influences we experience are our own unhelpful thoughts and feelings or those that are projected towards us from others, society and the environment. Much, if not most, of a healer's work is in this area. At times it is sufficient to clear this negativity and then help strengthen a person's energy field, so s/he has the space to work through what is going on and deal with personal issues rather than too many outside difficult energies. Negative energies tend to show up in all the areas of the subtle energy field, although they are mostly noticeable in the subtle layers and chakras.

Virtually all healers sense, see or know energy in a different way, which can be likened to a personal 'language'. Some perceive negativity as dark clouds or unpleasant feelings. Others, however, have a more dramatic view of things and can then mistake what is ordinary negative energy for something more sinister. This is fine, provided the healer knows what is what and does not communicate what they perceive to their clients, because this could frighten them unnecessarily. We also often draw what we fear towards us, which is why much attention must be paid to what is communicated to others concerning this.

Many years ago, there was a period when I was inundated with calls from terrified people, who had been told by healers that they had entities attached to them, or that they needed their homes cleared because dark energies were present and other similar scenarios. Several came to me for a session, and the only thing I had to do in virtually every single case, was reassure them. None had anything threatening within their energy field. There is no need whatsoever for a healer to tell a client that they have seen or removed dark issues, even if they believe this is the case. Unless there is a need for a referral, it will not help the client, and it shows a lack of sensitivity as well as questionable expertise.

There are also a number of people who believe that someone has cursed them. Although this does happen, it is not all that common, and unfortunately such fears have been exploited by unprincipled individuals, as is relatively well known. Removing curses is a specialist subject. The way this is dealt with depends on the culture and belief system of the person who is cursed, as well as the one who has done the cursing. There exist, however, family curses that have affected generations, and in such a case it is necessary to find the reason for the curse, and then take appropriate measures. There are also crystals and gemstones that are cursed and which are impossible to clear. The reasons for such curses must have been serious indeed, and these are often lost in the mists of time. All of the above requires expertise and does not form part of ordinary healer training. What you can do, if circumstances require, is to work together with an expert and after s/he has dealt with the actual curse issue, the client may well benefit from a healing session.

There is also the vast subject of what is termed psychic attack, including questionable magic, which has become fairly common, due to all the information available on the internet and in books. Psychic attack is the term for an individual deliberately trying to harm another by way of energy practices. This can range from life-threatening issues to mundane inconvenience, depending on the intent as well as the knowledge of the practitioner and the recipient of the attack. There is as much (if not more) warfare going on between people on the energy planes as there is on down-to-earth levels. Unfortunately, most of the unsavoury information out there does not include mention of the inevitable consequences of harming or trying to harm others. We are responsible for all that we do, and, although we can hide this and sometimes escape consequences in this world, we cannot do so in the energy planes. Balance is always restored, even if this may take a long time.

There are also many who dabble in darker forms of magic, without being aware of the dangers of this, and they can do much damage both deliberately and inadvertently. Some go and meditate in nature, opening doorways to ask for assistance from energies that reside there or because they are curious. Often such doorways are left open, and involuted energies can then freely enter this world, and harm those who live nearby or who are linked to such misguided folk. If such energies have been called forth to do the dirty on someone, this can become quite damaging to both victim and perpetrator. There are also people who use talismans or symbolism unwisely to the detriment of others and themselves; the list is endless. It is best not to engage in such practices, and ensure that all energy work one does is for the highest good of everyone, even if there is a nasty issue with another person and one may be sorely tempted!

For serious psychic attack issues, it is sensible to seek professional help. Word of mouth is the best way to do this, and there are also departments in most belief and religious organisations that deal with such negativity, especially the life-threatening issues. For yourself there are many ways to strengthen your energy field, as described elsewhere in this book. Ultimately, the most effective method is to reach such a high note that insidious energies, wherever they come from, cannot possibly enter your space. If you are aware of someone deliberately emitting negative energies towards you, you can return these, although a better option is to deal with what is yours and then make sure that the rest is deflected. This will either return to the person or go into the collective and, since you cannot possibly see the bigger picture, it is the wisest way to do this. If your client is undergoing some form of psychic attack, you can help by clearing and protecting their energy field and relevant chakras, and then teaching him or her a few methods of doing this for themselves. If you feel it is a nastier issue, it is imperative to refer to those who know how to deal with this.

Very dark energies, which relate to what I call the opposite of the Angelic, are unmistakable, and if a client is affected by these, the only way to help is to refer them to those who work professionally in this field. If you are facilitating a healing session and such a sinister energy comes to the fore, you have to bring both the client and yourself back into an ordinary state of awareness, after which you can have a chat and then refer onwards. This is very rare indeed and most healers will never come across it. There are few healers who are called to do such work since it requires not just an extraordinarily high link, but also an utter absence of fear. Equally, such folk are quite sturdy, since it can happen that they may have to physically fend off a client who is not in control. Most of them only do this for a few years since it is quite taxing. Virtually all religions and beliefs have specially trained people to deal with such issues, and it is not advisable to delve into this subject out of curiosity. If you do not have the name of a healer who works in this field, ask the client about their belief system and then advise them to seek help there rather than look at the internet.

If it happens (and this is very rare indeed), that you are personally confronted with such a sinister energy, you must not engage with it and should immediately ask the Angelic for help. You may also need to stop your work for a day or two and clear and protect your space and strengthen your energy field. When this happened to me once or twice, I just told the energies to buzz off and that I was not interested in a fairly forceful manner; then re-linked and asked for help which was always given. If you feel you need extra protection in your home with regard to this or similar issues, you can ask the four ArchAngel energies for help. In such a case, you would first link and then begin by facing the East and asking the ArchAngel Raphael for protection, followed by facing the South, West and North, asking the ArchAngels Michael, Gabriel and Uriel (in that order) for the same. Mentally connect those four points with a golden Light whilst you are doing this. It is an old and simple method that many Light workers have used in the past, and you will feel that it works. As mentioned before, you will only receive a tiny fraction of the mighty energies of these ArchAngels in question, and there is no need to see them, although it is always important to say thank you afterwards.

Years ago, I asked a colleague who worked in this field if I could accompany her in order to learn about it. I wanted to do this so I would be able to come from a point of experience rather than just theory, when I teach students on how to proceed. I was told to link, protect and only assist if asked. The whole experience was something out of a horror movie! Doors opened and slammed shut by themselves, lights went off and on, there were unpleasant smells and there was also a person there who had an unmentionable dark energy within them. My colleague dealt with all of this in a matter-of-fact way and did not need my help. I just observed and at some stage had a sense of the ridiculous, although I managed to keep my laughter silent. It showed me that humour is an excellent protection against negativity, and also that this type of work was not for me! This healer cleared the space as well as the person from this negativity, and then was highly reassuring, rather than pointing out what the dark energies represented.

Clearing spaces is something healers are often asked to do and most of the time this is quite straightforward. If, however, you become aware that something is beyond your abilities, please refer to those who are more experienced. There are also places in nature that are in need of clearing. If you are walking through a meadow or forest, it can happen that you feel an unpleasant change around you. It is advisable to then move on quickly, but once you have returned home you can offer Light to the area if you feel comfortable about it, as explained in the chapter on planetary healing. Please do not forget to keep your own home energetically clean as well. Healers are often so focussed on energy work for others that they forget to take care of themselves and their own space!

Frequent use of potent drugs and excessive alcohol weaken one's energy field to the point that our innate protection is destroyed. Virtually anything can then enter our energy fields, and the chakras become severely damaged. We advise to only offer healing to individuals who suffer from this if they also receive help from relevant organisations such as NA or AA. This also requires considerable experience and minimal use (if any) of crystals. In such instances, energy centres can be so damaged that intricate repair work is needed, after the addiction has been overcome.

As mentioned before, when developing as a healer, we raise our note. When at home it is perfectly OK to meditate and thereby expand our auric field. Doing this in a public place can have difficult consequences. Some folk may feel threatened by being exposed to a higher energy and get angry. I have known of healers who forgot to draw in their energy fields when going out and who were subsequently attacked.

My own experience, in my early years of training, was when one evening, a colleague and I were waiting for a train in an underground station in London. Out of the blue, a very angry man started to insult my colleague, calling her names and even threatening to throw her on to the rails. I do not think he meant it, but he sounded furious. I quietly asked the Light for help and think my colleague did the same. At that moment another man approached and started to have a go at the nasty fellow, telling him to back off or else. The angry man slunk off, our train quickly arrived and peace ensued. We did not even have the opportunity to thank our rescuer. A few years later I realised why this had happened and to date always advise my students to make sure to be in an ordinary state of awareness when going out.

24

Rescue Work

Rescue work is a term used by healers for a specialised form of energy work: namely, assisting those who have died under traumatic circumstances and not 'moved on'. As mentioned before, mediums and healers will often team up to tackle such a challenging issue. The medium will communicate with the trapped 'spirit', and the healer will help infuse the space with a high vibration and keep it protected. Usually, it is enough to link high and ask (the Light and the Angelic) for a being that is known to the unfortunate spirit to come and assist, and then channel energies as required. Do not do this type of work if you feel nervous about it.

Rescue work is also undertaken when there is a catastrophe somewhere. This includes war, earthquakes etc., or any occurrence where many have lost their lives. For this type of work, which involves such a multitude of people, you link to the Light, ask for healing energies to help with the situation, and then channel these for as long as necessary. Ensure you clear your energy field and ground properly once you have finished. A number of our experienced graduate healers meet from time to time and, when necessary, conduct rescue work of this nature. On one occasion, when intending to channel Light to a disaster area where a large number of people had perished instantly and unexpectedly, no energy was forthcoming. This was surprising and it is of my opinion, that many other healers around the world, may have been doing the same work (since the event was televised) and leaving our input unnecessary. Another possibility is that all those who died had made a soul contract before incarnating, had become aware of this at the moment of passing, and subsequently moved on with ease. Since then, in similar scenarios, Light and healing energies were always made available in plenty, so this was obviously a one-off.

A number of people who have died in hospitals sometimes continue to linger. Some may be unaware that they have passed away, others may be confused or are hesitant about moving on. Most living folk are unaware of this, and the energy is usually unthreatening. If you are highly sensitive, however, you may find it helpful to take a few precautions if you have to visit or stay in a hospital. You can do this by strongly affirming that you do not wish to be disturbed and ask your guidance and the Angelic for help with this. You could also take appropriate flower essences, such as the Bach Flower essence Clematis to help you stay grounded and Walnut to help protect your energy field. Crystals with grounding and strengthening energies are also useful.

An interesting phenomenon is that many healers frequently do this type of work while they are asleep. If (for no good reason) you often wake up more tired than when you went to bed, and you have vague recollections of helping people, you have probably been very busy in the energy worlds! If you need a break from this, just state before you go to sleep that you need your rest and do not want to participate. You can then just make sure your energy field is strong before you go to sleep. This is always honoured.

25

Respecting Boundaries

Virtually all conventional and alternative therapies are about healing as are most complementary and subtle energy therapies, although some substitute the word healing with wellness, well-being and so forth. It is therefore worthwhile to have a brief look at some of these in order to be able to maintain essential boundaries and to ensure your clients know what it is they are receiving. The vast world of therapies, at the time of writing, can be divided into the following four main categories:

Conventional Medicine is the domain of the medical profession. Practitioners diagnose, treat physical symptoms and also prescribe medication. Psychiatry, psychology and a few other related fields also form part of this. It is about treating illness directly, be this physical, emotional or mental.

Alternative Medicine is a word for therapies in which practitioners are able to diagnose, treat physical symptoms and prescribe herbal or other natural remedies. Homeopathy and Acupuncture are two of these therapies.

Complementary Medicine consists of many therapies, all of which complement conventional and/or alternative medicine. Practitioners do not diagnose physical symptoms nor prescribe medication, since they are not qualified to do so. A few complementary therapies, however, also address the physical body directly. Massage and aromatherapy are but two examples.

Subtle Energy Medicine consists of therapies where practitioners do not diagnose physical symptoms nor address these directly. They also do not prescribe medication, but instead, focus on and address imbalances that are apparent in an individual's energy field and the systems within this field. Crystal and energy healing come under this heading.

It is important for all practitioners in these therapies to respect the boundaries between them, and only offer those in which they are fully qualified. The word medicine does not mean medication. For all categories you could substitute the word medicine with the word therapy.

What to call your Therapy

Nowadays there are many different terms for what used to be called spiritual healing. A few of these are bio-field healing, energy healing, subtle energy healing/therapy, magnetic healing and vortex healing. When crystals or other tools are used, the terms for this are crystal healing, crystal therapy, gem therapy, electro crystal therapy, sound healing, colour healing and so on. This can be confusing for potential clients and the public at large.

Graduates of the Vibrational Healing Foundation (VHF), are qualified in both crystal and energy healing and also receive a certificate as a subtle energy medicine practitioner™. This is because the practitioner can work to a more profound level than usual standards set for crystal and energy healing, and is able to utilise a number of healing tools other than crystals. Practitioners who have then undertaken and completed an additional two years (or more) post-graduate training, which includes several extra qualifications, can use the term subtle energy medicine specialist™. They will always clearly explain to a potential client what their therapy includes.

What to call Yourself

There are also many different terms for the word healer. These include spiritual healer, energy healer or therapist, bio-field healer, metaphysician, Angel therapist, vortex healer, mystic, occultist, Shaman, Wiccan, Druid, Light worker, crystal healer, crystal therapist, colour healer, sound healer and many more. Over the last decade or so, many VHF students and graduates have told me that the word 'healer' no longer seems to be understood correctly and that many people believe that healers fix health-related issues. Through various internet searches, I discovered (at the time of writing) that they were right, and that the general consensus seems to be that a healer is someone who purports to aid recovery from ill-health. This is an imprecise description that could indeed lead to the notion that healers can fix physical symptoms.

I have often been asked if I could come up with a different word instead of 'healer' to describe what we do. Having reflected upon this, I personally believe the word 'healer' is fine, provided people understand what is meant by this, prior to booking a session. Words are powerful and, like anything else, open to distortion or not being used correctly. Changing a word because of this is not a solution, since the new definition could in turn be distorted, and so it goes on. Healing has existed for thousands of years in various forms, and as long as practitioners can clearly explain what they offer, there should be no problem with the words they use to describe themselves.

Those who are deeply involved in energy work, often call themselves Light workers (the capital L is used when a higher form of Light is indicated), and that is also fine. It just means that they channel healing and Light to others and the world, and are also active on the path of inner development. One could, of course, also call them healers! The bottom line is that if you want to call yourself a healer, you should briefly describe to a potential client (or anyone else) what that means.

Charging for Healing

There are healers who find it difficult to charge for their work, although most of these treat it as a hobby only, and may not have spent years in study and training. Others may have ample income and do not want to charge their clients, and it is also often stated that healers must do their work for free because the energies they channel are given freely. Although that is true, healers most certainly do not charge for healing energies. The notion of not charging could originate in the erroneous perception that healing is about religion, and that it was a God-given gift to only few individuals. I once heard someone say that Jesus of Nazareth did not charge, and that therefore healers should not either. All of this may have been valid once upon a time, but the world has changed since then, and I do not believe that any healers would compare themselves to this master healer and teacher. If anyone does, s/he could definitely benefit from addressing a few solar plexus issues. Healers, like other therapists, charge for their time and their skills only.

Some healers, however, participate in walk-in healing clinics, where short sessions are usually given on a donation basis; others may choose to wave their fee on occasion, and no healer I know would ever refuse help to a person who needs it. There are, however, several considerations with regard to charging for this work. First of all, although healing is a vocational profession, healers must pay their bills just like anyone else. Secondly, giving and receiving represents a balance. Many healers initially find it easy to give out, but difficult to receive, which is something that is often recognisable in their heart centre, where the energy flow going out is very strong but the energy coming in is blocked, which can cause issues. As already mentioned in chapter fifteen about cause and effect, the best way forward is to live in and create as much balance as possible, and even if tension is necessary to instigate change, it is preferable to do this in the most moderate way possible.

Another factor is that not charging a fee risks negating the innate value of this therapy. There is also the question of how much to charge, and our suggestion is to stay in line with what other therapists in your area charge. There is no point in undercutting anyone or charging fees beyond the norm, since doing so can create a negative vibration towards you and there is also the question of ethics. Many healers, in addition to crystal and energy healing, practise a second therapy that does not involve linking to and channelling energies, since doing this all day long can create an imbalance. Some healers do part-time work in more mundane professions in order to maintain a balance both financially and energetically. Although charging for healing is a practical subject, there has been much debate about it, which is why it is included in these pages.

PART II

ADDING CRYSTALS INTO THE MIX

26

Crystals and Healing

Crystal healing, as mentioned earlier in the book, is a highly specialised form of healing which can be viewed as energy healing with the use of crystals. Crystals are incredibly powerful tools, since they can shape and focus energies in every possible way, including amplifying, softening, strengthening, clearing, calming, grounding and so on. In addition to this, each crystal has its own specific energy which is due to its mineral content, inner geometry, colour and outer form.

Although one could say that wearing a crystal is wearing an energy, this has only slightly more effect than wearing anything else, and cannot be compared to crystal healing. If so, royals and wealthy celebrities could not possibly wear their stunning jewellery, since they would be unable to function in a normal manner. Healers rarely use gems of the high quality fashioned into valuable jewellery on their clients, because their energies are so much more potent than those of ordinary crystals. If such stones are used, this is always done sparingly, and only on those who can handle the intensity. Holding a crystal and then entering a profound meditative state can, however, be considered a self-healing method although this is very different from a crystal healing session.

There are many reasons why crystals are used in healing, other than their many qualities and energies. Since both the crust and the mantle of the Earth are mostly crystalline, and it has been suggested that the inner core consists of metals, it can be safely stated that we are living on a crystal. Rocks, stones and sand are partly crystalline and the seas and oceans are full of salt. Our physical bodies contain many minerals and trace elements, which indicates that we are partly crystalline. Crystals also play a large role in our life in the form of jewellery, building materials and technology. Crystals are the most orderly structure in nature, which I am convinced also has a part to play with regard to their powerful energies.

The mineral kingdom is the first that came into existence on our planet and is one of the building blocks thereof. Everything else is nurtured by this kingdom! Gemstones have always been, and still are regarded as objects of great value and the use of crystals in healing is by no means a new concept. The legend of Atlantis, (and there is always a modicum of truth in legends), states that crystals were widely used in healing, but also that its downfall was largely due to the misuse of power including that of crystals. With regard to the increasing amount of technology with which we are bombarded, and everything else that is going on, we can only hope that enough of us wake up so history will not repeat itself!

To come back to crystal healing, this valuable therapy, in a nutshell, involves placing crystals on and around a client where appropriate, then activating these as well as channelling healing energies where required. The following chapters discuss how this is done in more detail and a few fundamental techniques are indicated, in order to give the reader a greater insight into why it is advisable to embark on a serious study, if intending to practise professionally.

Preparing Crystals

It is essential that crystals that are used for healing are scrupulously clean on both physical and subtle levels. There are many methods of cleaning crystals and each healer has a few favourites. Healers link to the Light before cleansing their crystals, since this is far more effective than doing it without energy. When cleansing your crystals, you must hold this intent in your mind. You can sound a bowl or bell into a group of crystals, you can hold them under the tap, you can channel Light into them, you can hold them over incense or gently breathe over them (provided you do not have a cold). Please note that crystals that have a metallic content may lose their sheen if held under water and also that many crystals fade in strong sunlight. Equally it is not a good idea to place Clear Quartz that is polished in sunlight since this can cause fire.

During a healing session it may occasionally be necessary to remove a crystal from a client's energy field a second or two after placing it there, since it may have absorbed a huge amount of negative energy. If this is the case, you must either set it aside and use another one, or clean it using a fast method. It is best to use the breath or channelling Light for fast cleaning, since unexpected sound may disturb your client. When you remove crystals from a client's energy field, always ensure they do not 'contaminate' your other crystals, so place them a little away from these.

If you have experienced a shift in your own development, it is important to clean all your crystals and re-tune them, because you will be working at a different level. You cannot really clean too much, so the more the better!

Tuning crystals is done via thought and it is important to be linked (to the Light) when doing this, since the tuning is then of the right 'quality'. All crystals you use for healing work must be tuned for healing. It is as simple as that. When using them on a client, you then tune them 'for the highest good of the client' (thinking the actual name of the client) before you place them on or around him/her. This is the only thing you need to do. If your client needs clearing, choose a clearing crystal and tune it 'for the highest good of the client'. There is no need to tune it for clearing since it does this already. The same goes for grounding or any other activity. Just choose correctly and tune 'for your client's highest good and the crystals will shape and focus the healing energies according to need and in accordance with their own vibration. After the session you clear the crystals that were used and re-tune them for healing (in general), before putting them back in your kit.

Many call the tuning process programming. The reason this is not done in these pages is that programming indicates imposing one's will, whereas tuning is more of a 'fine-tuning' (with the help of a higher Light) of a crystal's natural energy. We act as a channel (for healing) for the highest good of a client. When using crystals, their natural vibration will shape and focus healing energies and thereby 'enhance' those energies to a more profound level. This is why, when we choose crystals correctly for a specific purpose, we only need to fine-tune them and not force anything. It is not a good idea to impose your will in a healing session by leaving out the 'highest good' part and then only focussing intently on the outcome that you believe is right.

You cannot possibly know the bigger picture with regard to another person's life and what you impose could well turn out to be detrimental in the long run. Some healers are able to eliminate minor physical symptoms by using their will, especially if they combine such work with powerful crystals. This is called magnetic healing. Since the cause of the symptoms in question is not addressed, however, they often re-appear. Connecting with a higher Light, including the higher self of your clients, then making sure the overall intent is for their highest good and well-being and then proceeding to the best of your abilities, is the safest and most responsible way of carrying out any form of subtle energy healing work.

In order to avoid damage to your crystals, place those that have an identical hardness together. There is a list of Mohs hardness of crystals in Appendix B of the book. Please also note that, should you have to travel with your kit, fragile crystals need extra careful packaging. There are boxes available that consist of several compartments with small partitions in each of these that can be used to transport crystals. Although not very appealing, wrapping your crystals in newspaper is the most effective way to protect them when you have to travel unless you have bubble wrap available.

27

The Energy Systems and Crystals

This chapter delves into a few ways in which you can use crystals on the subtle energy systems. The techniques are not described in a step-by-step manner, because those who read this book have already acquired, or are acquiring this knowledge and practice from their school. Intricate techniques necessitate a certain amount of (supervised) practical experience, and cannot be learned in theory only. This is the reason why only a few of the more fundamental techniques on the energy systems are included.

Subtle Bodies and Crystals

Crystalline energies can help clear, unblock, lift, calm and stabilize issues that may show up in certain levels in the auric field, and also help repair damage. This is possible to various degrees and according to the specific note of the crystals that are used. The personal energies of both the healer and the client also play a part in this, which is one of the reasons that no two healers will work in exactly the same way with a client. They would in all probability address different issues, especially if one is more used to addressing higher levels, and the other more down to earth levels in the client's energy field. Since healers are only able to channel energies according to where they are at in their personal development, it follows that this also varies and explains why healers rarely choose the same crystals for similar techniques. This is another reason for the fact that one can only generalise in the broadest sense of the word about the choice of crystals for healing purposes.

Healers often place their clients in a pattern of crystals, which relates to issues that are occurring in specific levels of their energy field. Such patterns are natural shapes such as squares, triangles ovals, circles, an equal armed cross or stars. All these shapes represent different energies that can enhance the healing process in accordance with what a client requires. The crystals that are chosen must also harmonise with the shapes in question. A square represents a grounding energy which is why grounding crystals are appropriate for this shape. Usually a square of small crystals is placed at the feet of a client, but if someone needs grounding on mental or inspirational levels, such a square can be placed around the person. In this case only crystals with a higher note, such as Lapis Lazuli, Sodalite or Fluorite can be used. Although of a high frequency, they have a grounding quality because their inner geometry is cubic and this shape relates to the element of earth itself. Please note that you must never place dense or grounding crystals around a person, since these are only suitable for the lower two chakras, lower gridlines and underneath the feet.

For the triangle shape, enhancing or energising crystals are used, since this pattern represents an uplifting energy. For circles and ovals, which are often used to strengthen someone's field, you can apply most crystals of a medium to high note and the same goes for stars and the equal armed cross. The five-pointed star epitomises a protective energy, so crystals of a high note are best for this shape, and the six-pointed star represents a spiritual shift (as above, so below) so crystals of a high note are also used for this. The choice of crystals must always be in accordance with what is going on at the specific level (or levels) one is working on, and also in accordance with the state of the client's energy field as a whole. It is best to keep it simple, and only use one type of crystal for most shapes. For an oval or circle, you can use two types of alternating crystals and the same goes for an equal armed cross, but the other shapes require only one type of energy.

Please note that some shapes can also represent religious beliefs, such as the five-pointed star epitomising a Wiccan or Pagan symbol and a six-pointed star relating to Judaism. Therefore, from an ethical viewpoint, it is necessary to ask a client before a session starts, if they would mind being placed in such a shape should this be required. Many years ago, when awaiting my turn in a healing clinic, I saw one of the healers draw a Christian Cross on the back of each of her clients at the end of the session. Before I left, I had the chance to speak to her and asked why she did this. She told me it was the most powerful symbol with regard to healing, and that she did this automatically without asking her clients. To me such behaviour is somewhat questionable, because I believe that we must respect people's religious beliefs, and not do anything that could relate to these without their express consent. This includes placing someone in a pattern that can epitomise a belief.

It can, however, happen that a person wants to be placed in a pattern that represents a religious symbol, although this is rare. I recall facilitating a session for someone who felt vulnerable because she thought she was under a form of energetic attack. I asked her what belief she adhered to and she told me she was Catholic, and when encouraged, mentioned that she felt the Christian cross was a highly protective symbol. I then asked her if she would like me to place her in this pattern and she was delighted with that so I did. It helped a great deal and I have no doubt that her personal belief played a part in the positive outcome of the session. This example illustrates that symbols carry powerful energies and why it is so important to use them with care.

Symbols that represent ritualistic or other forms of magic, sacred writings, talismans, or any other such energies, must not be used in healing others. If a healer is thus inclined, s/he will be aware of the exact meaning and potential consequences of using such powerful methods, and only do this for personal purposes.

A method to clear debris from the auric field is to draw an appropriate crystal through the layer or layers that need this. It is appropriate to use a smooth crystal for this although, in the case of more stubborn debris, this can also be done with a small Amethyst or Apophyllite cluster. This technique is usually used just once during a session, and again towards the end, in order to make sure all is clear. The energy of the crystal you use will not just clear but also introduce its specific energy into the layer in question. If it becomes apparent at the start of a healing session that the debris present in a client's energy field is preventing you from perceiving what needs to be addressed, you can clear the field with either sound or a crystal. In such a rare case, you would clear the field at the start, once during the healing and once at the end. Utilising this technique more often could result in a severe healing crisis, which you want to avoid.

Repairing a severely damaged auric field or levels within this field is specialised work and with regard to the scope of this book, I would advise not to use crystals for this, unless you are clairvoyant to a high degree. In such a situation it may be more appropriate to use flowers, flower remedies or just keep it to energy healing alone.

Chakras and Crystals

Placing a crystal on a chakra is always invasive, and this is the reason that this part of a session is usually done quite fast. If you have placed a client in a pattern of crystals, it may become apparent that a number of chakras also need to be addressed. The choice of the crystals that are used depends on the exact state of these chakras as well as the other crystals that form part of the session. Once the crystals are chosen, they are carefully placed on the chakras and then briefly activated with the healing energies. Crystals can help energize, calm, clear, ground and stabilize chakras to various degrees. They can also be instrumental in opening a chakra to a deeper level or slowing it down if this is required. Crystals can help initiate or integrate change, promote a finer link or even repair or re-define a chakra that is severely damaged. It all depends on what is going on and this work is complex. It is the main reason we always advise to do 'rather less than more' since too little only means less effective, but too much can result in unpleasant or worse consequences.

When you are introducing a crystal into a chakra, it will start to do its work as soon as it reaches the outer levels of that chakra. Sometimes you may need to hold it for a moment over the chakra, on a specific level, before placing it on the body. If so, hold it still, rather than move it over the chakra. You do not know if the overriding spin of the chakra is clock- or counter-clockwise, and if you get it wrong, this is unpleasant for the client. Holding it still for a few moments will accomplish what is required. It is also often at this moment that a crystal absorbs debris, so you may even have to remove it, before introducing a second crystal, which you can then place directly on the body.

After the crystals have been placed on the chakras and activated with healing energy, the healer will step back and channel energies into the whole of the field or, in some cases, just hold the space. To channel energies for longer than a moment into a chakra that has a crystal on it, is too intense and intrusive. Usually, working on three or four chakras is all it takes, and you would not place crystals on three chakras that are next to each other. The reason for this is that one of the three may only appear unbalanced because of the other two, and therefore does not need to be addressed. After a few minutes, the healer will, again with great care, remove the crystals from the chakras and continue with the session.

Using a set of seven different crystals is a technique that can be used if a person's system is in relative balance and each chakra only needs a little fine tuning. This is mainly appropriate if there is not all that much going on in someone's life, and the whole set must also reflect a specific theme. The reason specific chakra sets are rarely appropriate is because everyone is different, and what is fitting for one person can be counterproductive for another. Even if one uses seven identical crystals, these have to be chosen with great care, because this technique will flood someone's system with one specific vibration which is an intense experience.

Most crystal healers have an array of small crystals that they use for this type of healing and rarely use the same combination. With regard to chakra healing, it is equally important that all crystals used, including the grounding stones, are in relative harmony with each other. Crystals that are placed on chakras must ideally be of a similar size and, if working on only three or four chakras in one session, each of the crystals must have a different energy, because each chakra has a different spin. The base chakra spins slowest and the crown fastest, and if you work to create the best possible balance within a number of chakras, it follows that each of these requires a different energy.

Gridlines and Crystals

Gridlines mainly need clearing, unblocking, strengthening re-defining and in some cases it is a case of helping to create an overall balance in this system.

Always place identical crystals on either side of a line in order to address what is required. Tune them together, place them, connect them energetically and activate them. Crystals are always placed on the central vertical line, because this one anchors the whole grid. Do not work on more than two or three of the horizontal lines and never on three that are next to each other. If it is appropriate to address the androgynous lines, you need four identical crystals for these, and you would also place crystals on the vertical line. These could be either the same or of a similar energy. Crystals with a high vibration are mainly used for the androgynous, vertical and shoulder lines. Crystals with a lower note can also be placed on the other lines. The key, as always, is to make sure everything harmonises.

Please note that one can work on either the androgynous and central lines or the horizontal and central lines and not combine this. If you cannot perceive the grid lines, do not work on them. Also bear in mind that when you place crystals around a person, his or her energy field will expand, so you have to reposition them accordingly. The same goes for patterns.

During a healing session, when working on the gridline system, it can happen that the energy all of a sudden dramatically changes, and a healer becomes aware of the need to intensify the whole session. In this case s/he would first of all ensure that all the crystals placed on this system are identical. Certain geometrical shapes may then become visible in the energy field and there is usually a need to briefly and gently focus healing energy on one small area. It may also become apparent that all crystals must be connected around the client. This work relates to the highest aspects of a person and a healer usually only needs to 'hold' the space for as long as is indicated.

Please note that you can combine patterns as well as gridlines with working on chakras, ensuring always that not more than one crystal is placed over the crown chakra area.

28

Self-Healing Techniques with Crystals

This chapter consists of a number of self-healing techniques that are easy to implement. Ultimately all healing is self-healing, which is why, when nothing much is amiss in your life, you can enhance your experiences without the help of another healer. Please always ground yourself fully after these methods and also draw in and protect your energy field if you have to go out in the world!

Healing Meditation with a Crystal

This technique is powerful and should never be underestimated. You start by making sure you will not be disturbed. Then ground, centre, link to the Light and choose one crystal for your self-healing process and two grounders that harmonise with it. You then clear and tune the crystals for your highest good, ask to be a channel for healing for yourself and that the crystals may shape and focus the energies according to need. Place the grounding crystals underneath your feet and hold the other crystal in one of your hands. Then let the energies flow through and around you, in the knowledge that they will affect you where it is needed most. Fifteen to twenty minutes is enough time for this. Some people may fall asleep when doing this, so it could be beneficial to lie down rather than sit in a chair. Fully ground at the end or when you wake up and clean your crystals.

Clearing Meditation with Crystals

Choose seven crystals of a similar size that have clearing energies, tune them for your highest good and place them in a vertical line in front of you. Pale Smokey Quartz, Moonstone, Snowy Quartz, Apophyllite, Blue Topaz, Amethyst and Selenite would be appropriate for this. Place the Smokey Quartz closest to you and the Selenite furthest away. Ground, centre, link to the Light and then become aware of and connect to the Smokey Quartz and let the energies of this crystal surround you, clearing away any debris on your etheric layer, then focus on the Moonstone for the emotional layer and so forth until you finish with the Selenite for the last layer. After this, ask the Angelic and the Light to replenish your energy field with the appropriate healing ray. Do not forget to clean your crystals afterwards and of course to ground yourself!

Profound Chakra Meditation

There is no need to hold a crystal for this, although if you get spaced out when you meditate, you could place a couple of grounding crystals at your feet. This is an excellent way of gaining information about issues that may be going on in one of your chakras. Sit in a comfortable chair, ground, centre and link to the Light and your guidance and also ask that you may be fully protected during your meditation. You then enter your favourite landscape and, as you are walking along, you see a big building which you enter. You find yourself in a large rectangular room. Along the wall facing you are seven doors, which are fashioned out of crystals. Standing in the centre of the room, now focus on the first door at the far right of the wall. It is made up of fiery red Rubies that start to glow when you look at them. The energies of the Rubies reach you, and if you feel so inclined, you can let them enter into your energy field for a moment. Then take your focus to the second door, which is made up of bright orange Carnelians mixed with Fire Opals which start to glow and if you wish, you can let these energies briefly touch you. Then move to the third door, which is made up of bright yellow Citrines, mixed with Golden Optical Calcites, and when they start to glow, let the energies briefly touch you.

The fourth door right in front of you is made up of beautiful Emeralds. In the centre there is a circle, consisting of Morganites. The crystals start to glow and briefly touch you. The fifth door is a little to the left of the one in front of you and consists of Aquamarines and Blue Topaz crystals. The frame of this door is Silver. As you look at the door, the crystals begin to glow and briefly touch you. The sixth door consists of dark blue Sapphires. As you focus on it, the crystals glow and touch you briefly. You then have a look at the last door which is made of Amethyst, and the frame of this door is Gold. The crystals glow and touch you briefly.

You now look at all the doors and decide which one you wish to enter. If you are not sure, confer with your guidance. Once you are happy with your decision, step in front of the door and ask it to open, which it will. You then step through and see what happens. You may be taken on a journey, you may meet beings, maybe you stay in a room – anything can happen. Please note that when you want to come back, you only need to ask and you will be transported instantly to the place where you entered. When you leave your adventure, please close the door firmly behind you. Taking a last look at all the doors, you can see that the crystals have all reverted to their ordinary state. Walk out of the building, close the door, and come back into your personal space and fully ground yourself.

Whatever you have experienced behind the door you chose relates to the relevant chakra and one of its associated life experiences.

Protection with Crystals

If you have to go to a difficult meeting and you don't feel as strong as usual, you could place a photograph of yourself in a pattern of protective crystals, such as Lapis Lazuli, Amethyst, Hawks Eye or Turquoise to name only a few. Just choose the one that is appropriate for you. Also add a couple of grounding stones so you do not become floaty or spaced out. Alternatively, you can place your picture in an Amethyst Geode, tuned for helping you to keep safe, and place a potent grounding stone in front of it. Before you go to the meeting, make sure your energy field is as clear and as strong as possible. You can do this by imagining your auric egg around you, filling the space with a high energy colour and coating the outside also with a colour such as electric blue, gold, silver or turquoise. You then make sure that the bottom part of your egg is also beneath you in the earth. If you need to be highly focussed you could also take a specifically tuned small piece of Clear Quartz with you. You can also carry a protective crystal with you, but this technique is equally, if not more effective.

Crystal Mandalas

Mandala is a Sanskrit word the meaning of which is centre of circumference. In Hindu it means circle. The circle is an important symbol that has many associations. It relates to the oneness of all that exists, to the self, to the wheel, planets, chakras, cycles, wholeness and so on. The yin/yang is a circular symbol; stone circles were always created in the shape of a circle, and some cultures built circular dwellings. Mandalas can help to bring subconscious issues to light and are therefore a valuable tool for self-healing. They can be drawn, painted or made with pebbles, flowers, leaves, sand and also crystals.

The way to work with this technique is to ground, centre and link to your guidance and focus on an issue that you may wish to change. Then create your mandala by placing a number of (clean) crystals in a pattern, taking as long as you like. This can be any kind of pattern; you can even make shapes and place crystals within it or make a crystal picture. Once you are happy with it, make a few small changes. The reason for this is that you are in the process of creating a new pattern. You can then activate your mandala by channelling Light into it and dedicating it for your highest good. If you have placed it in a space where it will not be disturbed, you can leave it for a few days and then dismantle it.

Alternatively, you can dedicate the mandala for your highest good and briefly take it energetically into your energy field as a whole. In this case, make sure there are not too many crystals in the mandala, since you do not want to create a healing crisis. Never take a mandala directly into any of your chakras, since this is far too intense.

Crystal Essences

Few crystals healers create crystal essences, since they have all their crystals at home and can use these whenever they want to. What you can do, however, is infuse your water with crystalline energy. In my opinion, the most appropriate crystal for this is Aquamarine. The reason for this is that this crystal is hexagonal, which is similar to the geometry of a snowflake, the purest shape of frozen water. I do not recommend placing crystals in a glass or jug of water, since many have slightly toxic trace elements or metals within their mineral content. In the case of Aquamarine this is Aluminium. Another reason is that crystals may be chipped or so small that one risks swallowing them.

Another way to enhance water is to place it in a glass or other container and clear it with sound. Alternatively, you can channel energy into the water with the intent of clearing it. You then tune your crystals and place them around the container. If using Aquamarine, you could place a few small crystals in the shape of a six-pointed star around the water, draw in the pattern and then activate it by channelling energies into it. In this case, the intent would be to energize the water for your highest good.

Please note that you will be able to use most healing techniques that you learn on your course for yourself as well.

29

Healing Others with the use of Crystals

In crystal healing, a healer will first of all gain an impression of the overall state of a client. This will give him/her a preliminary indication of which type of crystals to use. Some people can handle strong energies, others are more fragile and every single person is different. After this initial impression, and when the client is relaxed, the healer will evaluate which system or systems in the energy field need work. Most of the time s/he will start by focussing on either the subtle layers of the field or the gridlines, because you can leave crystals that are placed around a person for much longer than on energy centres.

Crystals are chosen according to the state of the energy systems that need to be addressed, which requires an in-depth knowledge and experience of their vibrations. Not only must all crystals that are used harmonise to an appropriate degree, but there is also usually a 'theme' that needs to be adhered to. Such themes can be calming, grounding, clearing, energising, strengthening, protecting and so on. Once can combine two or in some cases three of these themes, provided 'opposite' energies are not incorporated during one session. This means you must not use energising crystals as well as calming crystals in one session. You would either focus on the calming or on the energising theme.

Equally if crystals of a fairly slow vibration are used in the field (other than beneath the feet) you must not use crystals of a very high note in other parts. Crystals mainly harmonise via their energy, colour, crystal system, and family they belong to. The reason the recommendation was made earlier to harmonise the crystals to a relevant degree, is that this also depends on the exact state of the client's energy field. Too much perfection could result in a major healing crisis and too little could be chaotic or not all that effective.

Another aspect of using crystals in a healing session is that the whole energy field is in constant movement. Placing crystals on or around a person, and activating these, can spark an acute emotional response. Suppressed memories of unpleasant experiences can come to the fore, thought processes can be triggered and so on. All this shows up in the energy field, which is why a healer must monitor carefully what is going on during a session and adjust the healing process, and sometimes crystals, when necessary. It is therefore essential that a healer keeps his or her eyes open throughout a healing session. If you have to re-link, that is fine, but closing your eyes for longer than a few moments is not a good idea. In order to get used to this, it can be helpful to practise meditation with your eyes open.

It is advised to only use the minimum number of crystals and techniques, especially when starting out and refrain from 'overdoing' things, since that can have adverse effects. The following case study illustrates this.

Looking at my client's energy field, the sacral, solar plexus and throat chakras were underactive, severely blocked and badly underactive respectively and there were also considerable blockages in the subtle layers on levels two, (emotional) three (lower mental) and five (causal). The field as a whole was fragile. I got the strong impression to address this session with caution, placed the client in a gentle, protective pattern and then proceeded to address the three chakras in question briefly with crystals of not too potent a vibration. After this I gently addressed the second and third level of the field but left the fifth alone. A week later the client returned and reported she had suffered several nightmares of having been attacked by a shark and subsequently drowned.

Looking at the field, although it was a little stronger, the first impression was of the severe blockage in the fifth layer. The three chakras were now all slightly underactive and the blockages in the second and third layers were less bad. This time, after having placed the client in a pattern of stronger protective crystals, I started by addressing the blockage in the fifth layer and subsequently cleared the field of emerging debris. I also gently cleared the second and third layers and placed a strengthening crystal on the solar plexus. A week after, the client reported that the fear of swimming had subsided and that she was looking to go on a trip where swimming with sharks was possible. This time the energy field only needed a little more clearing and energising which was done.

I later heard that the trip had been a great success and the fear of swimming (and sharks) was completely gone. All of this indicated that the fear must have been a memory of what is termed a 'past life'. Had I used more potent crystals and addressed layer five during the first session, this could well have resulted in panic attacks rather than bad dreams and shows the need for prudence. For those who are experienced, such a scenario is not difficult to gauge, but for newly graduated healers it may be different and take some time to get used to.

One of the reasons that healers tend to use too many crystals when starting out is that they are concerned about their clients not being able to sense any energy. It is not necessary for clients to sense energies, because healing can affect one in more subtle ways, and it is helpful to point out to clients before a session starts, that they do not have to sense anything. It is especially important to advise them when the session has come to a close. Often clients are worried that they will not be able to sense this and are then unable to relax.

Distant Healing with Crystals

Distant healing with the use of crystals is as powerful (if not more) than 'hands on' healing. The reason for this is that there are no distractions. It is, however, of the essence that you know your client is relaxed and in their own home before you start. If they are out and about, or driving a car whilst you facilitate a healing session for them, they could well become disorientated or lose control. There are healers who believe that they can ask the Angelic or their guides to ensure that the healing energies only reach a client when appropriate. This is something I find questionable because we are fully responsible for what we do on this plane. And if we carry out a distant healing session whilst our client is driving a car, we cannot point fingers at guides or the Angelic, if s/he is involved in an accident!

One example to illustrate how powerful distant healing can be, is when I asked a colleague if I could try out a distant healing technique on her, which involved both crystals and sound. I called her before starting and she lay down on her sofa. After having finished I called her again for feedback and she told me she could not move during the session because the energies were incredibly intense, although beneficial. Had she not been safely at home, this could well have turned out badly, and it was a valuable lesson to take on board.

Most of the healing techniques you are taught on your course can be used for distant healing. An easy way to do this is to draw a human shape on a piece of paper, link this to the client by writing their name on it and then carry out your techniques. You can also use a photograph and place this (or the drawing) in a pattern of crystals or work on gridlines. Do not forget to reposition crystals when you sense that the client's energy field is expanding. It is advised to keep chakra work as simple as possible and make sure you clear the client's energy field when needed during and also at the end of the session. For this form of healing, you can use small or even tiny crystals. After you have finished and grounded the client, you also clear the picture or shape that you drew as well as the crystals that were used.

The more you practise distant healing, the more you will be able to get a sense of your client's energy field and evaluate with ever more precision what is required. If you do it often, it is worthwhile to keep a special space for this work in your home. Some healers use coloured scarves if their client's overall energy field lacks a certain colour, but if this is the case, do make sure you include a complementary note. If flowers are indicated, you can place small petals around or on the client and you can also use a Tibetan bowl for clearing.

The best time to carry out distant healing is just before the client goes to sleep and, as mentioned before, always make sure you have agreed on a specific time for you to start. Distant healing does not take as long as hands on healing, which is why you need to adjust your fees accordingly.

30

Planetary Healing with Crystals

You can create crystal mandalas for planetary healing and these are potent indeed. You must therefore ensure that your intent is clear and positive and also understand possible implications. It is important to voice the intent correctly and finish by affirming that the energies of the mandala may be dissolved into Light once its work is done. Whenever you do such work, ensure that you are always linked to the highest levels you can reach as well as the Angelic.

You can also create a crystal mandala to help support those who may be in need in disaster areas of any kind. In this case you would start by meditating for a while on your intent and then choose your crystals intuitively, making sure the whole is harmonious. You would then activate it, voice your intent and offer the energies accordingly. Having powerful healing energy forms in the etheric, created by healers for the highest good of all, on which those in need can draw upon, can only be of benefit in today's world.

You can leave a crystal in a relevant place, having tuned it for the health and well-being of that area. You can throw a small crystal in a lake or river, having tuned it to help clear the pollution and bring back health etc. On a holiday in Greece, I walked past a bunker that must have been a remnant of the Second World War. The energies surrounding it were dark indeed, so I tuned one of the small crystals I always carry with me to help heal the energies as appropriate and threw it in there. Whenever that little crystal came into my mind, I channelled Light towards it. After a few years this stopped, so I presumed its work was done.

For this type of healing work, please remember that the world also acts as a mirror; therefore, if you wish for peace, start with yourself and that will make a huge difference in the world. Creating a mandala for peace is fine, provided it is done for the whole world and not just a specific country which is at war. Creating a mandala for harmony, will show up any disharmony, which is why it is better in certain scenarios to generalise rather than focus on one place only. The possibilities are endless and there are groups of healers who meet often in order to facilitate such Light work for the planet and Humanity as a whole.

31

Children and Animal Healing with Crystals

Toddlers are rarely brought for healing, but if they do come, and it is indicated to use crystals, the best way is to ask the mother to hold the child and then place an oval or circular pattern of crystals around both of them. Gentle crystals such as Shell, Amber, Mangano Calcite or Blue Calcite are the most suitable for this. You then let the healing energies flow into this pattern. When finished, gently ground the mother.

If a child needs a calming energy in his or her room, you could place a Blue Calcite there. A colleague, who is experienced with children has confirmed this, and the cooling as well as calming energies of Blue Calcite are softer than those of Blue Lace Agate or other crystals with a calming energy. All children are highly sensitive and instinctively know which energy is beneficial for them. You can therefore take a bowl of tumble stones, let the child choose one they like, let them hold it during the session, and give it to them afterwards.

When I used to attend healing shows, we always made sure to have a container full of small tumbled crystals on our stand, and 'little people' who passed by were invited to choose one of these to take home. In some occasions slightly older children were advised by a parent which crystal they should take, and invariably a little later on, most of these children came back and asked if they could exchange their crystal. From our perspective this was always appropriate!

It is advisable to only work with crystals on chakras of children older than twelve and who have reached the age of puberty, unless in exceptional circumstances. Even then, please tread very carefully. Techniques such as simple patterns or gridlines are usually sufficient, as is energy healing without the use of crystals. If you are qualified to recommend Bach Flower essences, these are suitable for all ages.

With regard to crystals, most animals respond best to rough, unpolished crystals that do not have too strong an energy. Calcites, Feldspars, Amber and Shell are most appropriate for animal healing. Some of the other unpolished crystals that are suitable for animals are Aventurine, Rose Quartz, Blue Lace Agate, Moss Agate and all the Jaspers. You can hold a crystal whilst channelling healing energies towards the animal or alternatively place a suitable crystal near their basket or box for a while. You could also clear their energy field with either a White Calcite or Snowy Quartz. Animals will move away or let you know in another manner if they do not want healing, and always indicate to you when they have had enough. I have come across several people in my life who could communicate with animals to a degree that most of us cannot, and also know of healers who only work with animals.

If an animal is sick and you suspect it may have taken on board something from their owner, you could place a picture of it in a pattern of protective crystals. You will then have to monitor carefully what is going on, since the owner may feel the need for healing as well. If such an owner is aware of the worlds of energy, you can make him or her aware of this scenario. If not, it may be best not to say too much and act to the best of your abilities and understanding.

If a much-loved pet is old, very ill and on the way out, it may just need 'permission' from its owner to let go. On one occasion when someone asked me for healing for an animal that was very ill. I placed a picture of it in an Amethyst Geode, tuned for the purpose of helping it for its highest good and well-being, and gently channelled healing energies towards this. A little later, a clear picture of this animal entered my thoughts and did not shift for quite a while. I meditated on it, and received a strong impression to take the picture out of the Geode because it did not want further healing. After removing the photograph, I called the owner and explained what had happened and possible reasons for this. Upon reflection the owner communicated to her pet that it was okay to let go and it died peacefully soon after.

If you have an animal that is old and ill, and you are full of grief because of it, the Bach Flower Remedy Red Chestnut may be of help to both yourself and your pet. Once the animal has gone, you could then take Star of Bethlehem to help cope with your loss. Although animals form part of a group soul, they are often seen (after they died) with their owners by clairvoyants. This is especially the case with dogs and cats which are also often sensed by the owners in question. It could be that the bond between the owner and the animal is so strong that the animal has not yet fully 'left'.

32

Crystals and the Elements

If there is an imbalance of elements in you or a client, you can use crystals to help remedy this. Although crystals and metals form part of the element of earth, they can also represent the other ones energetically. The denser grounding crystals and metals would be used to help promote the element of earth and it is interesting to note that the colour of Red Jasper relates strongly to the actual vibration of the Earth. Crystals with a high-water content such as Apophyllite and Opal, can represent that element, as can Aquamarine, Shell, Coral and Pearl. Carnelian, Copper, Sulphur, Sunstone, Golden Topaz and Citrine all have a fiery energy and relate well to the element of fire. Clear Quartz, Snowy Quartz and Blue and Clear Topaz can all represent the element of air. Higher vibration crystals such as Celestite, Selenite and Danburite are more appropriate to represent the element of ether. You could also take a symbol, such as a small crystalline statue of an Angel, to represent this element.

With regard to self-healing, you could fill a small container with earth, another with water, and also light a candle and some incense. Then place these objects around you and ask the Angelic to help balance the elements within yourself. More effects of the elements being out of balance within yourself and how to deal with this is described in chapter thirteen.

If you want to relate the elements to the four directions, earth relates to the North, water to the West, Air to the South and fire to the East. Some traditions place fire in the South and air in the East, but my understanding was given intuitively and after many years (to my relief) was confirmed by reading an extract of an ancient Druidic text. At the time of writing my amazing editor presented me with more confirmation and I will leave it at that. The element of Ether in this case would be in the centre.

We once facilitated a group healing to balance the elements and placed four healers in a square, each one representing an element, with the recipient of the energies sitting in the centre. The experience was intense but also very funny. Every healer, whilst channelling, felt the element they represented very strongly. The earth healers felt heavy, the water and air healers felt an urgent need to go the bathroom for relevant reasons, the fire healers started sweating and the recipients who were receiving the healing energies all felt a huge shift. We decided afterwards that it was more comfortable to use crystals or the actual elements themselves.

For clients lacking in earth, you could place a small square of earthy crystals at their feet; an oval of watery crystals if they lacked water; for a lack of fire, an upward triangle with fiery crystals; and a triangle with the tip pointing downwards for the air element. For the ether you could place the client in a six-pointed star if they were happy with this. In each of these cases you would incorporate one crystal representing each of the other elements. The client could hold these or you could place them within the actual pattern. Another method to balance the energies in this way is to place the client (if agreeing to this) or yourself in a five-pointed star. The top crystal would represent the ether and the other four the actual elements. In this case the crystals representing water and earth would be placed on the lower points of the star.

33

Colour, Sound and Crystals

Crystals come in many colours, but even those that have similar colours usually have very different energies, which is why one cannot generalise about this. Although chakras contain all colours, they have one overriding colour vibration. It is sometimes presumed that the choice of crystals on chakras is determined by this colour, but this is not the case. The following example illustrates this. The overriding colour of the solar plexus chakra is yellow. Citrine and Yellow Jasper are both yellow crystals. Citrine, however, has a highly energising and uplifting energy and Yellow Jasper a grounding and stabilizing energy. If you place a Citrine on an over-active solar plexus you would worsen this state and if you place Yellow Jasper on an underactive solar plexus, this would do no good. Furthermore, you could place Citrine anywhere in the energy field and on any chakra that required this uplifting energy. Yellow Jasper is too dense an energy to place higher than the solar plexus. For an overactive Solar plexus, Amethyst or Blue Lace Agate could be more suitable and for an underactive one Clear Quartz or Rutilated Quartz (if crystals of the Quartz family were indicated).

Another example concerning green crystals is as follows. Malachite, Aventurine and Green Tourmaline have very different energies although all three are green. Malachite is far too dense a crystal to place on the heart centre, Aventurine on the heart chakra would help gently strengthen it and Green Tourmaline has such a potent energy that it could only be used on the heart centre of someone with a strong energy field.

Even violet crystals cannot always be used throughout the energy field. Violet Garnet or Jasper, which you cannot place higher than the solar plexus and base respectively are examples of this. They also would not be suitable for grounding purposes and other than on the chakras mentioned, you could only place them on the two lower gridlines.

A further example with regard to crystals with the same or similar colours is that of pink crystals, which are often generalised with regard to the heart chakra. Rose Quartz, Pink Opal, Mango Calcite, Pink Shell, Strawberry Quartz, Rhodochrosite, Rubellite, Morganite and Danburite are all pink. Of all these, Pink Shell has the softest energy, followed by Pink Opal and Mango Calcite. Stronger energies are those of Rose Quartz and Strawberry Quartz and Rhodochrosite. Rubellite is extremely intense and Morganite and Danburite are of a much higher note. Rhodonite is mainly suitable for grounding or the base chakra and lower gridlines. Although pink, Rhodonite, most Strawberry Quartz and the majority of Rhodochrosite crystals are not suitable to place on a heart chakra or higher. Although you could use Morganite and Danburite anywhere in the system, their energies are mainly effective on the higher levels. Rubellite is such an intense crystal, it is only suitable for those who can handle this. Rose Quartz, which has a medium energy can be placed anywhere but it is not always appropriate to place it on a heart chakra. It all depends on the state of an individual's energy field and the state of chakras (and other systems).

You can, however, use crystals of any colour on chakras, provided their energies relate to the specific chakra in question. Black, dark brown, red or orange crystals are never used on the higher chakras or levels in the auric field.

At times it is indicated to use only one specific colour vibration on a client. This could be a pattern of Rose Quartz and other pink crystals. In such a case it may be appropriate to incorporate one or two crystals of a complementary colour, in order to balance this out. Green Jasper, Moss Agate or Green Garnet would be appropriate for the above example. You could use two Green Jasper or Garnet grounders or, alternatively, let the client hold a piece of Moss Agate. Complementary colours with regard to crystal healing are red and green, blue and orange and yellow and purple. This is the same as on the palette of artists that create oil paintings. In my time you only put red, blue and yellow (primary colours) and white paint on your palette. With these four colours you can create any other colour.

As mentioned before, you can use the sound of Tibetan bowls in combination with crystal healing. It can also be appropriate to take a piece of Clear Quartz and gently sound a note, using your voice, into the energy field of a client, who may have been placed in a pattern of crystals. There is no need to direct the sound into a specific part of the energy field; just sound it in general towards it and only once or twice. This will enhance the whole healing. The intent must be (as always) for the highest good of the client.

You can use sound for yourself by holding a piece of Clear Quartz, tuned for your highest good, and hold it whilst you chant vowel sounds to enhance your chakra system. You could also tune a crystal to help you chant or speak mantras or your affirmations. In the latter case, you may prefer to use a different crystal, more in harmony with the actual affirmation.

Another way to use sound is when you create a mandala, either for yourself, or for planetary healing and, after having voiced the intent, you can chant into this as appropriate.

A self-healing technique using sound is the following: When you are healthy and in top form, which could be after a holiday or a few days off work, place yourself in a pattern of relaxing crystals, attune to the Light and ask that you may be a channel for your personal health and well-being and let the healing energies flow right through and around you. Then record a relaxation exercise that lasts around ten minutes. You could go through your main body parts, relaxing these, or just create a meditation of your own, in a beautiful garden or landscape. Whenever you feel out of kilter, listen to this recording which may well help you restore balance. The reason this works is that it is your own voice and energy, in an optimum state of health, that you are listening to which is far more effective than listening to someone else! Alternatively, you could place yourself in an energising pattern of crystals and record an uplifting exercise.

You can also use your voice to clear you space whilst holding a crystal. In this case the intent, whilst you chant or sing, is that of clearing and the most suitable crystals for this are Snowy Quartz, Blue Topaz or Apophyllite. These are a few indications only on how you can combine crystals with sound for yourself, and you can always be creative and experiment! Please just remember to always ground at the end of an exercise, unless your intent is to fall asleep.

34

Various Crystal Shapes

Crystals are often fashioned into shapes such as wands, spheres, cubes or pyramids. They can also form naturally in such shapes (except the sphere). Clear Quartz wands, Pyrite cubes, Fluorite octahedra and small pyramid-shaped Apophyllite pieces are all natural. Most healers, however, use fashioned shapes. Since shapes already represent a specific energy, crystal ones are used with care. A crystal sphere is suitable for holding in front of an energy centre, since chakras move in a spiral-like fashion and the shape of a sphere harmonises with that. A wand can be used sideways (horizontally), in order to help clear layers of the energy field, and those who can clearly and accurately perceive chakras may use a wand to clear or repair these if this is indicated. A pyramid represents a heightened energy and, depending on the type of crystal, a small pyramid can be used on an energy centre in order to help initiate considerable change. A cube represents grounding. Most healers have a few spheres and wands in their healing kit.

Many crystals are currently fashioned into skulls. It is believed by a number of people that twelve crystal skulls were created out of Rock Crystal, by people from another civilization. This was done to store information about their civilization for the future. I think this is extremely probable, but do not believe that newly-fashioned crystal skulls are similar. They can, like any other crystal, be used in meditation and both the crystalline substance and the shape will add to such inner work. A piece of Quartz, fashioned in the shape of a human head, can definitely help activate certain parts of our brain if that is our belief and intent. Those proficient at profound energy work, however, are able to link to any type of information without the need for crystals or other tools.

Cut and Polished Crystals (and Cats)

There is a significant difference between polished and unpolished crystals. Polished crystals have a (slightly) more intense vibration than the natural variety because, when polished, more light can shine through. If they are also cut, the difference is considerable, as one can see in gemstone jewellery. It is interesting to note that Shamanic healers, who are all close to nature, prefer the use of unpolished or rough crystals. Their healing methods are of a more physical nature and also affect the body more directly. Such healers often use herbs, drums, rattles and even animals in their work. I once worked with a Shaman from the very north of Europe. She told me she cleansed her crystals by drawing them through the fur of her cat. Not knowing much about cats, I asked her if this was not detrimental to the health of the cat. She said that cats (not kittens) thrive on negativity and a number of cat owners later confirmed to me that this is indeed the case.

A few years ago, I was in the company of a person who was unwell, and we sat down on a bench. A cat appeared out of nowhere, jumped on my friend's lap, then jumped off and was violently sick. It obviously was aware of the unpleasant energies that were present in my friend and chose to do something about it. If you have harmful ley lines in your garden or home, your cat may be happy to lie on or near these and ants also do not have a problem with this form of negativity. The reason I am including these stories, is that a number of healers have told me that their cats have a tendency to jump on clients during a session. If you have a cat, I would strongly advise you to ask clients if they are OK with this before the start of a session! Dogs seem to respect boundaries a little more and are on the whole averse to any kind of negativity, although they will take it on board from their owners in order to help them.

Crystal Systems

Crystals are the most orderly structure in nature because their atoms are arranged in a regular geometrical pattern. All crystals can be grouped into seven different systems according to their inner geometry. Some of these systems are more regular than others and of the seven, the cubic system is the most regular and the triclinic the least regular. There are also minerals that have no regular inner geometry and crystal system.

Healers must be mindful of the actual crystal systems of the crystals they use for several reasons. Being aware of the inner geometry of crystals can help to harmonise those used in a session and crystals that do not have an inner regular structure, usually have a less intense energy. Another reason is that we respond strongly to shapes. If we place a client in a shape that mirrors the shape of the crystal system of the crystals that are used, the whole session intensifies. Placing someone in a six-pointed star of Aquamarine, will have a more profound effect than doing this with Clear Quartz, although the latter carries a more intense energy. The reason for this is that unlike Clear Quartz, Aquamarine is hexagonal, which mirrors the shape of a six-pointed star.

Below is a list of shapes, a few qualities these can represent and relevant crystals.

The **cubic** shape in 2D is a square which one can relate to earthly issues such as grounding, stability, security, strength, manifestation and so on. You can place a square at a person's feet if s/he is lying down, or alternatively at the feet of the chair they are sitting on. For a square, grounding crystals are used. If you wish to place a square around someone, you could use cubic crystals that are of a higher vibration, such as Fluorite, Sodalite or Lapis

Lazuli. You could then use grounding crystals such as Garnet or Copper, which also are cubic. Some other cubic crystals are Diamond, Halite, Pyrite, Copper, Silver, Gold, Galina and Spinel.

The **tetragonal** shape in 2D is a rectangle. This shape can represent more mundane human issues. Our houses, rooms, beds, tables etc., are mostly rectangular. It stretches a little further and is more fluid than the square. It is quite a comfortable shape for us since we are so used to it. Some of the tetragonal crystals are Apophyllite, Scapolite, Rutile, Zircon and Vesuvianite. There are not all that many tetragonal crystals that are used in healing work, the main one being Apophyllite which has a clearing quality.

The **monoclinic** shape in 2D is a parallelogram and is slightly more dynamic than the rectangle. It is the start to a slightly higher vibration and could represent a quality of starting to be a little less traditional or looking for something new. It also relates to starting to balance energy and matter in a more knowledgeable manner. A few of the many monoclinic crystals are Moonstone, Selenite, Azurite, Malachite, Jade, Kunzite, Unakite, Epidote, Lepidolite and Charoite.

The **orthorhombic** shape in 2D is like a diamond shape or a square tilted on its side. This is a more active and dynamic shape than the square, rectangle or parallelogram and therefore has a higher note. It is also more balanced that the monoclinic shape, which could indicate becoming a little more comfortable with innovative issues. If one were addressing the androgynous gridline and a client could handle such a potent 'double whammy' these crystals could intensify the experience. Some of the many orthorhombic crystals are Topaz, Danburite, Prehnite, Iolite, Zoisite, Sulphur, Dumortierite, Aragonite and Celestite.

The **trigonal** shape in 2D is a triangle which on more profound levels could represent aspiring to a higher unity, also an awareness that we are a soul that is having an incarnation here on Earth, rather than our body having a soul. There are very many trigonal crystals. The Quartz, Calcite and Tourmaline families are all trigonal and so are Rhodochrosite, Ruby, Sapphire, and Hematite.

The **hexagonal** shape in 2D is a hexagon. It is the shape of a six-pointed star which is composed of two intertwining triangles and therefore more balanced than the triangle by itself. This star also represents the maxim 'as above, so below' which one could relate to gaining a much deeper understanding of who we really are. There are not all that many hexagonal crystals. The Beryl family, Sugilite and Apatite are those used in healing. Ice, provided it is not polluted, also has a hexagonal shape as can be perceived in snowflakes.

The **triclinic** shape in 2D is a trapezium. It is the most irregular shape of the seven systems and therefore can indicate a need for change or someone being in an acute state of change. It can also relate to promoting flexibility or releasing old patterning. The crystals that belong to this system are a little different from the norm and have a more profound, magical or intense energy. Labradorite, Sunstone, Oligoclase, Amazonite, Kyanite, Turquoise, Rhodonite and Astrophyllite are all triclinic.

Although not a crystal system, it is worthwhile to include the crystals/minerals that do not have a regular inner geometry. These are called **amorphous** and one could, at a push, relate this to the shape of a sphere. Many of these crystals are used when a softer approach is needed. Most of these are glasses or organic substances such as Obsidian, Moldavite, Amber, Copal, Jet, Coral, Pearl, Shell, and Opal. Some of these are only partly amorphous, but their energies are so gentle that this is not of great importance.

35

Different Formations of Crystals

Most Quartz crystals form as clusters with six-sided prisms with pyramidal terminations. At times there are slight differences which also affect their energies. Below is a list of a few that are often used by healers.

Double Terminated Crystals

Double terminated Quartz crystals have pyramidal terminations on each side of the prism rather than on one side only, when they are called single terminated crystals. In healing they can be used when you wish the energies to flow both ways and are therefore often used as a bridge.

Elestials

Elestials mostly form as Clear Quartz, Smokey Quartz or Clear Quartz with Epidote. They look as if their points are embedded in the structure of the crystal. With regard to energy, Elestials are powerful crystals that can be used to bring to light deep-seated issues, which is why they are mainly used by healers for self-healing purposes. If you place a large Elestial in your home, the energies within it will change considerably and with it your life, especially if you practice any form of energy work.

Laser Wands

Laser wands are ancient crystals that look a little worn and that do not have the spark of ordinary Clear Quartz prisms. They are either Smokey or Clear Quartz and are incredibly powerful.

They can be used to draw protective symbols, such as five- or six-pointed stars around oneself. They can also be used to help clear persistent blockages, provided the healer can perceive these clearly and is experienced enough to know how much (or how little) can be done safely.

Lemurian Crystals

These are Quartz wands that have horizontal striations on all six sides. The striations look like small ladders. These crystals are only suitable for personal meditation and accessing information about our world and the various civilizations that have lived on it. There is also information about the crystal kingdom itself, although this is only released to those who are ready for this.

Phantom Crystals

Phantoms are Quartz crystals whose growth stopped several times over millennia and this process shows up as several layers within such a crystal. Energetically they can relate to our own growth processes and healers mainly use phantoms for personal meditation.

Record Keepers

Record keepers are crystals in which one or more tiny triangles are present on the pyramidal terminations of Clear Quartz prisms. These triangles can appear at any time and often only do so after one has acquired one of these crystals. These crystals hold information that is often important to their owners and therefore these crystals are mainly used in meditation.

Tabular Crystals

Tabular crystals are Clear Quartz crystals that rather than six equal-sided prisms have two main flat ones. The other four are very small. These crystals can be used to help clear the energy field but have no specific other meaning.

Twinned Crystals

Twinned crystals are Clear Quartz clusters that consist of two prisms that have grown together. In other words, 'double trouble'! They are also used in meditation or self-healing when one needs an extra boost of energy.

Window Crystals

Window crystals have a diamond shape that connects two of the six sides of a Clear Quartz prism. Many believe that holding this diamond shape over one's brow chakra promotes clairvoyance. In my personal opinion it is a good crystal to meditate with, especially if seeking answers to certain questions.

36

Crystal Qualities

Since this book is about both crystal and energy healing, the use of crystals and their energetic properties are much elaborated on. Although crystal healing can ultimately affect physical well-being, as explained a few times elsewhere, this is done in an indirect manner and therefore physical symptoms are not included. I have also not added many suggestions for use with specific emotional or mental qualities such as 'good for anger' or 'good for confidence'. The reason for this is that where the energies of one crystal can be of help with an issue for a certain individual, the same crystal may be utterly ineffective for another. Anger, for instance, could relate to an over-active solar plexus and confidence to an under-active or blocked solar plexus, which is what a healer must focus on rather than the actual emotion.

Equally, when qualities such as nurturing, calming or energising are stated, this is meant to be in a general fashion. One example of this is Blue Lace Agate, which can relate to calming. Holding a Blue Lace Agate in cases of stress, over-worry or anxiety, may help some, but it could be counterproductive for others. For some individuals grounding crystals would be more suitable, others would need a more stabilizing energy and so forth. It all depends on what is going on in the energy field of the person. Therefore, if such qualities are mentioned, this is only meant as a description of the energies in the broadest way possible, and for the healer to be able to start to familiarise him/herself with crystals with more ease.

With most of the crystals I have indicated where in the energy field they can be placed. There are, however, exceptions to 'the rule', so please take all of this as rough guideline only. I have also grouped most crystals in 'families' because their energies harmonise to a great degree. There are many crystals that cannot be grouped in this way although they also combine well with others and this has been indicated as much as possible. Again, please take this also on board as a very general guideline. I have depicted a number of ways of combining different crystals in patterns etc., and must repeat that this could be right for some and wrong for others. All of it is meant to help you start out and cannot be taken as gospel.

In books or on the internet there are many stories about crystals that are highly creative, Angelic, soul-like, imaginative and so on, which are probably the result of meditations and personal experiences of the authors. In order to keep it all as 'down to earth' as possible I have avoided such imaginative language and by no means wish to state that anyone is mistaken. Subtle energy therapies are in their infancy and it is, in my view, extremely important to promote the uniqueness of every Human being and avoid over-generalisation with regard to the use of crystals.

Although the book *Crystals & Healing for Everyone* also has a crystal list and a few pages with pictures, this is mainly meant for newcomers. I am elaborating to a larger degree in this book in relation to actual healing work, which is why there may be a slight difference from what is included in that booklet. For those who want pictures of crystals it is worthwhile to obtain an encyclopaedia of crystals or one or two books on gemmology. Most crystals are also pictured on the internet in ways that are far more diverse and recognisable than can be done in a book on healing.

A great number of crystals are included in the list, and it is not necessary for healers to acquire all of these, especially since some of them have similar energies. Crystals that are most often used in healing are a variation of grounding crystals, an array of Quartz, Feldspar and Calcite crystals, a smaller number of crystals with stronger energies, and a few that are very gentle. Most healers initially do not have more than a few hundred small tumbled stones and a selection of bigger pieces as well as a few gems and specifically-shaped crystals in their crystal kit.

It has to be mentioned, however, that the longer you are working in this field, the more crystals will find their way to you. All crystal healers love crystals, and their healing kits usually consist of a far greater number than are necessary for their healing practice! As long as you use your crystals for the benefit of your clients, yourself and the world at large, there is nothing wrong with having a large collection. I wish you much joy with your crystals, healing work and journey towards ever greater Light.

37

List of Crystals

THE QUARTZ FAMILY

Quartz is one of the two most common crystal families on the planet. The other is Feldspar. Most of the crystals that are sold commercially belong to the Quartz family, such as Citrine, Amethyst, Clear Quartz, Rose Quartz and Agate. The variety of crystals belonging to this family is enormous, and every crystal healer will have a sizeable number of these in their healing kits – not just because they are so plentiful but because they are suitable for almost everyone. The overall 'note' or energy vibration of Quartz crystals can be viewed as medium to high, and the potency is wide-ranging from hard to softer energies and from energy amplifying to grounding. The only people for whom Quartz could be considered too intense are those who are very fragile, elderly or very young. Quartz is found worldwide and comes in many colours. Its crystal system is trigonal, and the hardness is seven except for Herkimer Diamond which is slightly harder.

CRYSTAL FAMILIES

CRYSTAL FAMILIES continued

OTHER CRYSTALS

Amethyst

Amethyst has a relatively high vibration and can be used anywhere in the energy field. Its colour ranges from dark to the palest purple. If heated, either artificially or naturally in the earth, its colour transforms to a golden yellow and it becomes Citrine. When heated to an even greater degree it turns pale green and is then named Phrasiolite. Sometimes a crystal contains both a purple and golden hue in which case it is called Ametrine. The darkest variety of Amethyst is found in Uruguay and the palest, also called Vera Cruz Amethyst, is found in Mexico. Amethyst found in Russia often has a pronounced reddish glow within the purple.

Crystals usually have more than one energetic quality, and in the case of Amethyst this is both protective and clearing and therefore it is often used to help with regard to negative energies. It absorbs these, and needs extra cleansing when utilised in this manner. It also has what many perceive as a more spiritual vibration. This indicates suitability for the higher chakras, outer layers of the energy field, more intricate patterns and higher gridline work. Applied in this way, Amethyst would aid in establishing a deeper awareness. Where chakras are concerned, although it can be placed on any of these, Amethyst relates most to the crown and brow centres. It is often used as a meditation crystal and some find it helps them to fall asleep. In the case of Ametrine, this crystal would add an enhancing quality.

Aventurine

Aventurine comes in a variety of colours such as blue, peach, pale red and light to relatively dark green. Green Aventurine, which is the one most often used by healers, contains tiny specks of Mica which give the crystal a sparkle. This crystal personifies balance and strongly relates to nature. It can also be viewed as a complementary note to Rose Quartz. It is suitable to help balance stressed or overactive energies but it can also slightly strengthen underactive ones, depending on the actual situation and the energetic makeup of the client.

The lighter green variety can be used anywhere in the energy field. Aventurine is one of those crystals that are very often used, because their energy can be likened to 'middle of the road' energy. It is suitable for virtually any technique and combines beautifully with Petrified Wood grounders although most other grounding crystals can also be used. If a more intense grounding is required, Garnets also combine well with Aventurine.

A keyword for this crystal is stability, and it may be useful for the student to have another example of how to put seven green crystals together, to place on chakras if a person is in need of stability. As mentioned before, the whole system must be more or less in balance, and the overall state of the person's energy field should relate to the energies of the crystals used. In this case from base to crown, possible crystals could be Green Jasper, Epidote (or Unakite that is mostly green), Moss Agate, Aventurine, Green Fluorite, Prehnite and Hiddenite. To complement the green, the grounding crystals could be Rhodonite or Red Jasper and for a more intense session, Red Garnet.

Blue Lace Agate

Blue Lace Agate has both a clearing and calming energy. Its colour is a light blue with slightly darker striations. It personifies the quality of peace and is often used to help address stressed or overactive energies. If an energy field (which is not too fragile) needs both clearing and calming, one could combine Blue Lace Agate with Snowy Quartz in a pattern, since these crystals work beautifully together. One could then ground this with a crystal such as Botswana Agate, which has a similar but slightly denser energy. It is useful to meditate with Blue Lace Agate when feeling overwrought, although there are also softer as well as more profound crystals suitable for this.

Blue Lace Agate can be used anywhere in the energy field and on all the systems. You would, however, not use it if energising crystals also form part of the session.

Botswana Agate

Botswana Agate is a stunning grey crystal with brown and white stripes. Each crystal looks different and it is mainly used as a light grounder. It also has a clearing quality and can be placed on the base or sacral chakras and lower gridlines for this purpose. It harmonises extremely well with Blue Lace Agate and also Snowy Quartz for a clearing and slightly calming energy. It is an excellent crystal to meditate with when there is a need for change.

Botswana Agate also comes in a pink colour with white or grey stripes and this has a slightly higher note than the brown variety. One would use it in the same way although not for grounding purposes.

Carnelian

Carnelian comes in a pale to deep red orange colour. It can serve as a grounding crystal and is also used to address the two lower chakras or gridlines in a strengthening capacity. Although also thought of as a protective crystal, it cannot be placed around a person because its energy is too dense. Carnelian can relate to an energy point called the Hara, which is situated behind the sacral chakra. This is an area where martial artists centre themselves, and it is virtually impossible to push such people around, physically or otherwise! It is also a point where you can centre yourself for profound meditation and Carnelian is highly suitable to assist with this.

Carnelian relates well to the sacral chakra itself. If you feel a little vulnerable and have to go to a difficult meeting, Carnelian is one of the crystals that can help you be confident and stay well grounded! If you want to be more creative in a more mundane fashion, this energy is also appropriate. A brown variety of Carnelian called Sardonyx has a slower vibration and is mostly used for grounding or the lowest gridline.

Chalcedony

Chalcedony can be viewed as a gem-like variety of Blue Lace Agate and has a beautiful blue, basalt-like colour. This crystal, unlike Blue Lace Agate, has a fast and intense energy and when placed on a centre would give it a bit of a blast rather than calming it down. It harmonises better with crystals that have a higher frequency than most Quartz crystals, except for Herkimer Diamond or Clear Quartz which have a similar note. If Chalcedony is used in a session, deep red Carnelian, Hematite or Garnet are some of the more suitable grounders.

Chrysoprase

Chrysoprase is the light green variety of Chalcedony and a stunning crystal that can be placed anywhere in the energy field. Its energy is light and playful and mainly used in combination with other green crystals. At times it has Tourmaline inclusions in which case it cannot be placed on higher chakras or gridlines.

Like many green crystals it relates to nature, especially to the abundance of it, and therefore also represents this quality. In is enhancing and slightly uplifting and its energy is a little more intense than that of Prehnite but less so than blue Chalcedony.

Citrine

Citrine is a golden to pale-yellow crystal that is highly energising and uplifting. It also comes in a deep brown; in which case it has a more grounding effect. The golden variety personifies the quality of abundance for many. You could also compare it to a ray of sunlight. Most Citrine available on the market is (artificially) heated Amethyst, but this does not impede its energy. Natural Citrine is rare and therefore very expensive. This crystal can be used anywhere in the field where enhancement is needed.

Like Amethyst it can be placed on any of the energy centres, although it relates most to both the crown and the solar plexus. On an underactive crown chakra, it can have the effect of strengthening one's link to the Light. On an underactive solar plexus, it would create more of an energy of joy and radiance, rather than strengthen it. On more profound levels it can also relate to the heart chakra, which deepest colour vibration is gold. Citrine should, of course, never be placed on an overactive chakra, or used if a calming and releasing energy is needed. If used for the quality of abundance, it is worthwhile to look at why there is lack in your life. Depending on what is going on, other crystals could prove to be more suitable.

Clear Quartz

This crystal can be regarded as a master crystal, because it is so versatile. It shapes energies mostly in an amplifying manner, although it can also direct, link, drain, energize, focus, transmute, transform and shape these. It can be placed anywhere in the field and on any of the systems, if such a potent energy is appropriate. It must not be regarded as a crystal that clears energies since it mainly has an intensifying and highly energising effect. It can, however, dispel stubborn blockages in a somewhat blasting manner which is not suitable for everyone.

Clear Quartz is also an excellent crystal to use for studying in which case you can tune one to help you remember what you learn, as well as aid you to express this information when required. You can carry it with you whenever you are studying and during the relevant exam. Combined with a grounding crystal this works a treat for most! Many also use Clear Quartz as an aid to link to certain vibrations, meditate or to enhance the energies in the home. Clear Quartz is also one of the crystals that are used most in technology. Many healers, if told they can only have one crystal to work with, would choose Clear Quartz.

Fossilized Wood

Fossilized Wood, also named Petrified Wood, is part of an ancient tree that has turned into Quartz. It serves mostly as a gentle grounder and, if of a light colour, can be used throughout the energy field. People who are close to nature and to plant energies love this crystal. It goes well with almost all green crystals, and if a gentler choice of crystals is indicated, with Amber. Fossilized Wood can also contain Opal, in which case it is called Opalized Wood. This is extremely rare and more a collector's item rather than a crystal used for healing purposes.

If you have to work with a client who is fragile but needs nurturing, placing him or her in an oval of Amber with Fossilized Wood to ground would be a possibility.

Meditating with a piece of Fossilized Wood can be quite a surprising experience. You are linking to both the plant and mineral kingdoms and, although the main quality is that of grounding, it is also of transformation. It can therefore be helpful if you are going through a state of change.

Jaspers

There are many different types of Jasper. The main ones used in healing are Red Jasper, Green Jasper, (also named Heliotrope) and Yellow Jasper. All of these have a (medium) grounding quality. Red Jasper is a little more intense than the others. It is interesting to note that its terra cotta colour relates to the overall vibration of the Earth. Green Jasper is best used as a grounder if a more mellow energy is needed and the yellow variety has a stilling quality and can be quite helpful on an overactive solar plexus chakra. It is, in fact, the only Jasper I would use on a chakra higher than the base. Although all Jaspers can be used on the lower two gridlines, it is usually appropriate to place them on the lowest one and to keep these crystals for grounding purposes only.

Mookaite

Mookaite is a Jasper that is found in Australia. Its energy is a little gentler than the other Jaspers and it comes in a red-brown to pale yellow colour and sometimes violet. Each crystal looks different, and holding one may well help you to ground and stay calm when required.

Orbicular Jasper

Orbicular Jasper also called **Ocean Jasper,** is a Jasper from Madagascar which used to be mined from a place near the sea. Each crystal looks different, and it comes in virtually all colours and contains small patterns. It can help with stress on every single level, according to its colour vibration. The mine is now closed but another source of spectacular Jasper has been found on the island which is called **Polychrome Jasper**. Each piece of this stunning crystal is unique and looks a little like a modern painting. The overall energy provides a gentle grounding. Holding it can also help calm stresses.

Moss Agate

Moss Agate is a deep green crystal, combined with white or blue areas. It has a slightly denser energy than Aventurine and, like many green crystals, relates to balance and to nature. It beautifully complements both Rose Quartz and Strawberry Quartz and is not used on the higher levels of the energy field or the higher energy centres, except when very pale. It is an excellent crystal to meditate with when stressed or for a tense client to hold during a healing session. In this case you could also combine it with Blue Lace Agate or Snowy Quartz to help clear any blockages, as always depending on what is going on in the client's energy systems.

Moss Agate can be placed on the lower three gridlines and if you want to place your client in an equal armed cross, you could place Rose Quartz, Blue Lace Agate or a similar energy on the vertical bar and Moss Agate on the horizontal one. Petrified Wood combines well with it as a grounding crystal

Herkimer Diamond

Herkimer Diamond can be viewed as the most intense crystal of the Quartz family and the one with the highest note. It is mainly found in the United States in County Herkimer near New York. The reason for the name is that this crystal has a greater brilliance than the clear variety. It actually dazzles and is not all that often used together with other Quartz crystals, since it is more in harmony with higher energy crystals. Its hardness is 7.5. The energy of this crystal is on a par with cut and polished gemstones, which is why Herkimer Diamonds must be used with great care in healing work.

Rose Quartz

One of the key words for Rose Quartz is harmony. It has a nurturing but firm energy and is softer than the clear or milky variety. It can be underestimated, because it is more powerful than its colour suggests and not always suitable for a fragile energy field. One can say that it enhances in a moderate manner, but it can also soothe energies that are too intense. You could place a small Rose Quartz crystal on the under-active heart chakra of a client whose energy field is fragile. Alternatively, you could place a pattern of Rose Quartz crystals around a client whose energy field is too forceful. In one case the crystal strengthens and in the other it softens. It is all about matching energies.

Rose Quartz can be used on all the energy centres, layers of the field and gridlines, which makes it a highly versatile crystal and it is a must for a healer's crystal kit. The colour of this crystal also plays a large part in its energetic qualities. For some reason, it is impossible to stay angry for long if one is surrounded by pink, and aggressive behaviour, as well as fear, often relate to the solar plexus. In such a case this chakra would display an overactive or anxious energy, and one of the crystals that could make all the difference is Rose Quartz. In this scenario, it would help to calm the energies of the solar plexus as well as rebalance them. It is, however, always important to assess carefully what is needed and to avoid a massive healing crisis by overuse of crystals. Although Rose Quartz is mostly crystalline, it also forms in small clusters. The energy of these is more potent than the crystalline version.

Rutilated Quartz

Rutilated Quartz is Clear Quartz with inclusions of Rutile that look like golden, or golden- brown needles. It is even more potent than Clear Quartz and can be used anywhere in the energy field, provided the recipient has a robust overall energy. Rutile is tetragonal, which is different from Quartz and it comes in both grey and golden colours. The combination of two different crystals as well as two different crystal systems gives Rutilated Quartz that extra dimension.

Smokey Quartz

Smokey Quartz is a powerful crystal. Its colour ranges from a pale translucent brown to almost black. It is a crystal that is naturally irradiated in the Earth. Unfortunately, it is also often irradiated artificially and to perceive the difference with the naked eye is virtually impossible. I have the fortunate (although not pleasant) ability to detect artificially irradiated Smokey Quartz since I feel physically sick when I hold one of these. When acquiring a Smokey Quartz crystal, it is advised to ask the seller if it is natural or irradiated. It is important to avoid using artificial Smokey Quartz for healing, because the non-natural radiation affects this crystal's energy badly.

Smokey Quartz, if dark, is used for grounding, and the paler variety can be placed anywhere and is strengthening, especially with regard to dealing with negative energies. This includes deep inner fears or phobias, but if doing this, it is advised to also use other crystals such as Amethyst and/or Snowy Quartz or a gentle crystal such as Rose Quartz for its softer energy. One can, of course only do this with clients who are able to handle such intense work. Smokey Quartz is often used for personal meditation, inner development and to counteract geopathic stress.

Snowy Quartz

Snowy Quartz, also called Milky Quartz, is a crystal that is mainly used for clearing purposes. It has a medium vibration and can be used anywhere in the energy field, including all the subtle layers and chakras. With regard to the subtle layers it is, however, more appropriate for the etheric, emotional and lower mental levels. For the other levels it is more effective to use clearing crystals with a higher note, depending also on the actual state of a client's energy field. Snowy Quartz is a must for a healer's crystal kit. A few tumbled stones for creating patterns and chakra work, a few larger pieces for gridlines and a small sphere for addressing blockages in the energy field should suffice.

At times it is necessary to combine crystals, either in a pattern or even on gridlines. This is when two qualities are needed such as clearing and calming, or clearing as well as nurturing etc. Snowy Quartz is one of the most suitable crystals for the clearing part for this way of working, provided its vibration is in harmony with the other type of crystal you are using.

Strawberry Quartz

This pink crystal has a slightly slower vibration than that of Rose Quartz. Some of the crystals contain small grey or black inclusions, in which case they cannot be used everywhere in the field. Some feel that this crystal represents self-love, which is a quality many healers lack a little. An example of this would be heart centre energies that are strong and balanced with regard to emitting energies outwards but that lack this on the intake. Strawberry Quartz can help strengthen such a weakness, provided it does not contain the darker inclusions. If a number of different pink crystals are required in a session, on not too high or profound levels, a combination of Rose Quartz and Strawberry Quartz and grounding this with Rhodonite is great. If you then also hold a green crystal such as Aventurine, you create even more harmony.

If a person's energy centres are more or less in balance, and a pink nurturing vibration is indicated for each of them, you could use seven pink crystals from the base to the crown, consisting of Rhodonite, Rhodochrosite, Strawberry Quartz, Rose Quartz, Pink Opal, Mangano Calcite and Morganite. You could then ground this with either Green Jasper, or if a more intense energy was required, Green Garnet. The common denominator of the crystals would be the colour pink, and the green coloured grounding crystals would beautifully complement this. This only serves as one example on how to create a set, which would also have to relate to the overall state of the person's energy field, as well as the exact state of each chakra, even if these are only slightly out of balance.

Tiger's Eye

Tiger's Eye is a yellow and brown striped crystal. It has a slow energy and in healing work is mainly used for grounding. It also has a protective and strengthening quality, but on mundane and practical levels rather than more subtle ones. It is suitable for the two or three lower energy centres or grid lines, and must not be placed around a client. It can help with self-esteem, and if you need this quality you could carry it with you. Red Tiger's Eye is mainly heat treated and, if natural, only useful for grounding.

Tiger Iron

Tiger Iron is a combination of Red Jasper, Hematite and Tiger's Eye. It is a heavy-duty grounder and on a par with Black Tourmaline with regard to this. If someone with a strong energy field is in need of grounding, rather than using Tiger Iron in a healing session, you could suggest they carry a piece with them.

Hawk's Eye

Hawk's Eye is a deep blue, almost black variety of Tiger's Eye. It has striations of a slightly lighter blue colour and can be placed anywhere in the energy field, including the brow chakra. Its energy is protective in the way that it can help ward off negativity. It can also serve to avoid persistent nightmares, especially if these are the result of an unprotected energy field.

For a protective theme there is not much more harmonious than placing someone in a pattern of Hawk's Eye with Tiger's Eye grounders. Hawk's Eye also often has Hematite inclusions, in which case you would not use it on the higher levels or energy centres in the field. There is also a crystal called Pietersite which contains both Hawk's and Tiger's Eye and which is quite dense. Like a few other crystals, it can be helpful to carry when needing a little strength and protection but it is rarely used in a healing session.

Tourmilated Quartz

Tourmilated Quartz is Clear Quartz containing small inclusions of Black Tourmaline (also called Schorl). These inclusions give the Quartz a grounding energy and can therefore only be used on the lower levels of the field. This crystal can serve as an aid for meditation because it will help to link to both the Light and the Earth. It is also useful when you want to manifest a project because the Clear Quartz will help to keep you focussed and the Schorl will help to ground it all.

THE FELDSPAR FAMILY

Feldspars are the second most common crystal on the planet after Quartz. Their overall energy is not only more subtle than that of Quartz but it can also be more profound, especially that of Labradorite and Moonstone. The hardness of most Feldspars is around 6 on the Mohs scale and they belong to either the triclinic or the monoclinic crystal system.

Amazonite

Amazonite has a light to dark blue-green colour and is triclinic. It has too dense an energy for the heart centre but can be placed on the throat and is mostly used in combination with other triclinic crystals and Moonstone. It also combines well with Clear Quartz, Rose Quartz and Snowy Quartz. Its energy is strengthening and it can promote creativity, in which case it could be used for either a slightly blocked or and under-active sacral or throat centre. It can be placed on all the gridlines except the vertical and androgynous lines.

Labradorite

Labradorite grows in layers, and the reflection of light on these results in a blue, green, yellow and pale orange 'schiller' effect. It is a beautiful crystal and its energy is profound and magical. If placed on an energy centre, it can unlock deep-seated patterning, and it is also a crystal that promotes inner vision and therefore can be helpful with meditation. This crystal is triclinic and like all such crystals can signify the need for change, or being in a state of change. Subtle, deep and opening are keywords for this crystal, as well as mysterious and enchanting.

Labradorite can be used anywhere in the energy field but is especially suited to the brow and throat centres. If you want to escape the world for a while and go to a place of fairy tales, beauty and magic, meditate with a piece of Labradorite but make sure you also have strong grounders so you can come back with ease. Carnelian, Copper,

Pyrite, Jaspers and Garnets are a few of the grounders that go well with this crystal.

Moonstone

Moonstone comes in a variety of colours such as white, pale orange with white streaks, grey and black. All Moonstones have a white or silvery sheen and the best quality, also used in jewellery, is called Rainbow Moonstone which has a blue lustre. The crystal is monoclinic and its energy is fluid, subtle and can be viewed as feminine. It can be used anywhere in the energy field and is especially helpful for frazzled or stressed energies.

Moonstone also has a clearing energy which is more subtle than that of Snowy Quartz. Some find it helpful with regard to intuitive development and use it to promote clairvoyant and clairaudient abilities. Although it can be placed on any of the energy centres, it is often used on the sacral, throat or brow centres. Black Moonstone is intense and can bring deep inner fears to the fore, so must be handled with care. This type of Moonstone is mainly suitable for meditation.

Sunstone

Sunstone is a deep orange brown with a golden sheen as well as tiny Hematite inclusions which give it a sparkle. Its energy is denser than that of Moonstone and Labradorite and it can therefore only be used on the three lower energy centres and gridlines. It is triclinic and goes well with other crystals of this system, especially Turquoise. The energy of Sunstone is strengthening and it is often used on an underactive solar plexus which can relate to self-esteem issues. It is also a suitable crystal for the sacral chakra. Where Moonstone would gently clear this, Sunstone would strengthen it and Labradorite unlock blockages.

These three crystals work beautifully together because all of them have a magical quality. A slightly lesser quality of Sunstone is Oligoclase which has a golden sheen. Although not as profound or potent as Sunstone, it can be used in a similar fashion.

Sunstone should not be used by itself in patterns, because its energy is too slow to place above the crown. You can, however, combine it with either Labradorite or Moonstone, if it is appropriate to use more than one crystal in a pattern, such as an equal-armed cross. You could then place the Sunstone on the horizontal bar of the cross and Moonstone on the vertical one, in a case of balancing yin and yang energies. Hematite is one of the many grounding crystals that combines very well with Sunstone, since it already forms part of it.

Unakite

Unakite is a pink Feldspar with green Epidote and it is monoclinic. It has a slower energy than Moonstone and has a balancing and gently strengthening effect when placed on a chakra. You can also use it as a gentle grounder. The two colours complement each other beautifully and although pink and green relate to the heart centre, Unakite energy is too dense for this chakra, and is mostly used on the base, the sacral or the lower gridlines.

THE CALCITE FAMILY

Calcites come in many colours and are of both an opaque and a translucent variety, the latter of which is called Optical Calcite. Ordinary Calcites have a softer energy than Quartz and are less subtle than the Feldspars. They are often used for those who find other crystals too intense. Their energies, although not harsh, are quite firm and must not be underestimated. Different coloured Calcites have different energies. They are all trigonal and have a hardness of 3.

Red Calcite is a gentle grounder and can be used on the base chakra and lower two gridlines.

Orange Calcite has a warming and uplifting energy and can be used on the three lower gridlines and the three lower chakras.

Honey Calcite is soothing and has a slightly stronger energy than Amber. If very pale, it can be used throughout the energy field.

Pink Calcite, also called **Mangano Calcite,** is one of the gentlest pink crystals and is appropriate when Rose Quartz would be too potent.

Green Calcite is gently strengthening and, like a number of green crystals, has a stabilizing energy and can be helpful with stress and tension.

Blue Calcite has a cooling energy and can be of help with fraught and feverish energies. It has a much softer energy than Blue Lace Agate and is one of the few crystals that are suitable to place in a small child's bedroom

.

White Calcite, even if slightly translucent, has a softer energy than Snowy Quartz and is mostly used for gentle clearing. All of these Calcites can be placed anywhere in the energy field.

Black Calcite is rare and only used as a grounding crystal. **Septarian** is fossilized mud with yellow Calcite. This crystal is mainly used as a gentle grounder.

Optical Calcites

Optical Calcite has a much faster and intense energy than its opaque counterpart. It is useful to compare the first with an Angelic energy and the second with that of a Human Being. It also has a finer and slightly higher vibration than Quartz. Optical Calcites are mainly used in combination with other high energy crystals. The golden variety is mostly used in patterns or on higher gridlines in order to uplift and enhance the energy field. It is available as tumbled stones and these can be used above the crown centre and, in those who can handle this, on the heart or the solar plexus, provided the other crystals used are of a similar note. Clear Optical Calcite has a potent and amplifying energy, and is mainly used on higher gridlines or, on rare occasions, in simple patterns. The light pink and green variety are as intense as the other two, and must also be used with care.

There also exists a darker golden Optical Calcite, called Dogtooth Calcite, which is rare and therefore very expensive. In the healing world this is sometimes called Stellar Beam Calcite. It also comes in a white and translucent form and may contain Hematite inclusions. This crystal is mainly used for meditation or self-healing and has a powerful warming and uplifting energy.

THE BERYL FAMILY

The Beryl family has a more profound and far-reaching energy than the Quartz family, although its energies may seem similar on first impression. The inner geometry of this family is hexagonal which may account for the difference. The hardness of all Beryls is 8.

Aquamarine

Aquamarine, which in Latin means 'water from the sea', has a pale to dark blue colour. It is extremely versatile and can be used anywhere in the energy field. Its energy can be described as refreshing and clearing. Aquamarine combines well with many crystals. Together with Snowy Quartz it would enhance the clearing process, with Shell, this would be gentler and more fluid and with Clear Quartz the energies would be both clearing and amplifying. It also combines well with almost all crystals of a higher note.

Aquamarine is often used in patterns, especially the six-pointed star which correlates with the hexagonal crystal system. To place it in an oval around a person would refresh and boost the subtle energy field. Although it can be used on all chakras, it relates most to the throat. Carnelian, Red or Green Jasper, and Fossilized Wood are suitable grounders as well as Garnets if one wishes to intensify the session. Aquamarine is a must in a healer's kit.

Emerald

Emerald is one of the four crystals that are regarded as precious gemstones. The other three are Ruby, Sapphire and Diamond, although not all that long ago, high quality Tanzanite was added to this list. Polished high-grade gemstones that are fashioned into high-grade and valuable jewellery, are rarely used in crystal healing, since their energies are extremely intense when combined with channelled healing energies. If they are used, this is mainly on one of the chakras, provided the recipient can cope with such a concentrated energy.

Emerald has a beautiful green colour and is considered one of the classic crystals for the heart centre. It is often fashioned into engagement rings, surrounded by Diamonds. Energetically it would enhance a chakra in a much stronger fashion than a crystal from the Quartz family. The rough variety often contains black inclusions in which case it can only be used on lower parts of the energy field and on lower centres. If used in a pattern such as an equal-armed cross, it could be combined beautifully with Morganite on the vertical and Emerald on the horizontal bar. Garnets as well as other more potent grounding crystals go well with the energies of Emerald.

Golden Beryl

Golden Beryl, comes in a deep to pale yellow colour and can be used throughout the energy field. If one compares Aventurine, Rose Quartz and Citrine with Emerald, Morganite and Golden Beryl, the difference between these two families becomes obvious. The energies of Quartz are more direct and almost harsh compared to the more subtle but far-reaching energies of the Beryl family.

Morganite

Morganite is a pink Beryl which is similar to Rose Quartz although more potent. It can be used throughout the energy field and has an enhancing, almost opening energy.

It is, of course, highly complementary to Emerald and also the other Beryls. Where Emerald represents the overriding colour vibration of the heart chakra, Morganite takes this to a more profound and subtle level. Ultimately, however, it is Golden Beryl that relates to the most profound levels of the heart chakra.

Morganite also combines well with other powerful crystals such as Watermelon Tourmaline, Danburite, Kunzite, Peridot and many more. It is mainly used on a person who can resonate with intense and profound energies, even if they are subtle. For newcomers it is usually more appropriate to use crystals of the Quartz, Calcite and Feldspar families.

There are four more different coloured Beryls, which are not used all that often which is why they are not mentioned separately. These are:

Heliodore is a yellow/green coloured Beryl.

Goshenite is a clear Beryl which looks like Clear Quartz.

Bixbite is a red Beryl which is rare.

There also exists a **Black Beryl** that has no special name.

CORUNDUM

Corundum is the family name of both Ruby and Sapphire. Their inner geometry is trigonal and they have a more solid energy than the Beryls and are more intense than Quartz. The hardness of these crystals is 9.

Ruby

Ruby is considered a precious gemstone and is often seen in valuable jewellery, including the crown jewels of many Royal houses. Its colour ranges from a vibrant, deep red to a light pink. In healing it is mostly used on the base chakra and lower two gridlines. It is a less intense grounder than Red Garnet but more intense than Red Jasper. Ruby has a strengthening as well as a fiery energy that can help restore one's 'get up and go', relating to everyday life. In this case it would be used on an underactive base chakra, provided the person could resonate with this potent energy.

Although many consider Citrine to be the stone that promotes abundance, this is not necessarily so for everyone. Ruby, being such an important gemstone, obviously relates to abundance as do many others. It also depends on where in an individual's energy field there is an issue that blocks his/her abundance.

Sapphire

Sapphire comes in many colours but the best known is a dark blue. It is also considered a precious gemstone and often fashioned into engagement rings and other jewellery. In healing work Sapphires used are usually of a slightly paler blue than the polished gemstone variety. Blue Sapphire can be used anywhere in the field, although it relates strongly to the brow and throat centres. It has a profound, opening and also enhancing energy and relates to inner vision as well as wisdom.

The brow and base chakras strongly interrelate and if both need a strong energy, Blue Sapphire and Ruby would harmonise beautifully on these centres. In such a scenario, there are usually one or two other chakras that are a little out of kilter and one would then select crystals for these that carry as potent a note as the ones on the brow and base.

THE GYPSUM FAMILY

Gypsum crystals have a much softer vibration than virtually all other crystals, with an average hardness of just 2. This means they can be scratched with a fingernail. The crystal system of Gypsum crystals is monoclinic.

Alabaster

Alabaster forms in masses and is usually orange, green or brown. The orange variety is remarkable and has a softer as well as a more subtle energy than Carnelian. Alabaster is not used much in healing work, but is worthwhile to mention and include in a healing kit, in order to combine it with the other Gypsum crystals. It could be used to enhance a sacral chakra if Carnelian is too harsh, or used on either of the two lower gridlines if Satin Spar is used on others.

Desert Rose

Desert Rose is a flower shaped crystal that is either brown or brown combined with a white colour. It is in fact crystallised Sand, and can be used throughout the energy field. It is suitable for more gentle healing work and, although one cannot possibly describe this crystal as having a grounding energy, it is sometimes used to anchor Selenite (when a piece of Selenite is placed on the crown centre, Desert Rose could be placed on the base if not much work was needed there).

Selenite

Selenite often forms in pieces with jagged edges and is then called Fishtail Selenite. Fishtail Selenite is sometimes cut in half, which can be done with a sharp knife. In this case one of the sides is smooth and has a mother-of-pearl-like glow. Selenite also forms as blade-like, elongated flat crystals. The colour is a transparent white, grey or smoky black, although the latter is rare. Selenite has a very fine energy and tumbled stones of the white variety are mostly used on the crown centre or in high level gridline work in combination with other crystals. The blades are used to help clear the outer levels of the energy field and in meditation this crystal is often used to help link to the Angelic or similar high energies.

Satin Spar

Satin Spar is less transparent than Selenite and forms like shining white fibrous masses. It is often fashioned in pencil shapes or blades as well as tumbled stones. Like Selenite, it has a gentle clearing energy and enhancing energy. The chakra it mainly relates to is the crown. It can also be used for gridline healing if all the other crystals are of a similar nature and on the higher levels of the auric field.

THE GARNET FAMILY

Garnets are amongst the most widespread minerals and come in many types and a large variety of colours. All Garnets are cubic and can be divided into two groups, namely Pyralspite Garnets and Ugrandite Garnets. Both of these groups are subdivided into other groups that are in turn subdivided into different types of Garnets. The best-known high-quality red Garnets are Pyralspite Garnets which were often fashioned into jewellery in Victorian times.

Garnets are mainly used as grounding crystals on the two lower gridlines or the two lower chakras. They are far too dense to place anywhere else in the field, even if a pale colour. In view of this only a few are mentioned. The hardness of Garnets varies from 6.5 to 7.5 on the Mohs scale.

Black Garnet

Black Garnet, called Melanite, is suitable for heavy-duty grounding. It is only appropriate for those who can handle major and intense energies. Meditating with Melanite, will, more often than not, bring up profound inner shadows. This is the case with many black crystals, which is why these must not be used lightly. Melanite is, however, far more potent than black Moonstone or Obsidian, because unlike these two, it also has a transformative energy and is therefore more 'direct'. In a sense this is a crystal of deep magic (of the beneficial variety)! Some, however, call it the sorcerer's stone.

Green Garnet

There are many varieties of Green Garnet. The ones mostly used for grounding are green Grossular Garnet or Transvaal Jade, which is a green Garnet with tiny black inclusions. A Green Garnet used in jewellery is called Uvarovite and found in Russia. Although much lighter in colour it must not be used higher that the sacral or (at a push) solar plexus chakras. Green Garnets are slightly less intense than the red variety but they will also transform a session with more 'ordinary' crystals into something else!

Red Garnet

A type of Red Garnet called Almandine, which is a lesser quality than Pyrope, is mostly used in healing. Garnets have a highly transformative as well as potent energy, and must therefore not be used lightly. If used as grounders, they change the whole healing to a more intense level. This can be illustrated by the following example. If you were to place a client in an oval of Rose Quartz with Wood or Jasper grounders, this would provide a lovely nurturing energy. If one were to use Garnet grounders instead, the energy of the whole pattern would become far more intense and thereby deepen the whole session. An orange Garnet called Hessonite Garnet, is often fashioned in jewellery and can be used on the base and sacral chakras.

Garnets also come in yellow, pink and purple colours and these are also often fashioned into stunning jewellery.

SPODUMENES

This crystal family consists of **Hiddenite** and **Kunzite**. These crystals have a high and fine energy and their crystal system is monoclinic. Their hardness is 6.5 – 7.5.

Hiddenite

Hiddenite has a clear colour with a green tinge although sometimes the green colour is more pronounced. It has a complementary energy to Kunzite and both crystals work well together. It often forms in a wand-like structure which is suitable for clearing the energy field on higher mental or spiritual levels. Both Kunzite and Hiddenite can be used in a pattern around a person in order to help address issues on these levels. With regard to grid work, these crystals are often used on the androgynous lines. If this is the case, Garnet grounders are most appropriate.

Kunzite

Kunzite comes in a pale lilac colour with a pink hue. Its energy, like Hiddenite, is appropriate for the higher levels of the field higher chakras as well as the gridlines. It has an opening and flowing energy and although it has such a high note, it is suitable for anyone who is in need of a 'spiritual' lift or who has lost a sense of beauty and inspiration. Meditating with this crystal can indeed transport one to the experience of beauty, insights and higher visions. If someone is placed in a pattern of Kunzite and medium to strong grounders are needed, Malachite would be excellent, especially since it is also monoclinic. For something more transformative you would use Green or Red Garnet.

TOPAZ

Topaz is another powerful crystal. It comes in clear, blue, gold and pink colours and its crystal system is orthorhombic. The pink variety is often fashioned into valuable jewellery and the other three are mostly used in healing. The hardness of Topaz is 8.

Blue Topaz

The energy of this crystal is fast and somewhat blasting. Where Aquamarine can be likened to water, Blue Topaz is more like ice. It is sometimes difficult to distinguish these two crystals, although a give-away is that Blue Topaz is much colder to the touch. Both Clear and Blue Topaz can be used anywhere in the energy field, although they are more appropriate on higher levels such as the crown and throat areas. Clear Topaz has a harder, even more intense and blasting energy than that of Clear Quartz.

Blue Topaz can be used in patterns and on the higher gridlines if much clearing is needed. The chakra it relates most to is the throat, but in certain circumstances it can also be used on the solar plexus, sacral or base. Its energy is far too harsh for the heart or brow chakras of most people, and it is definitely not a crystal to be used on a fragile energy field. Blue Topaz is often irradiated but, unlike Smokey Quartz, this seems not to affect its energies. Carnelian, Copper, Hematite and Garnets are suitable grounding crystals to use with Blue Topaz.

Imperial Topaz

This is the golden variety of Topaz, sometimes with a pink hue. Unlike Blue Topaz it has a warming energy and it is mainly strengthening and, to a certain point, uplifting. It can be used throughout the energy field and works extremely well with other orthorhombic crystals such as Danburite and Peridot. If you place someone in a simple pattern of Golden Topaz and ground this with Copper, this is warming and enhancing. With Garnet grounders, the energies of this pattern would intensify. You could, of course, also use other grounding crystals. If you compare Golden Beryl with Golden Topaz, it is the Topaz that has a more potent energy and the Golden Beryl is more subtle and far-reaching.

Pink Topaz

This crystal is mainly available as expensive jewellery and, although called a semi-precious gem, it is definitely on a par with Rubies, Sapphires or Emeralds. The energies of Pink Topaz, Morganite and Rubellite with regard to a heart chakra are different in the way that Pink Topaz would open this centre up on the higher levels in a powerful fashion. Morganite would do this in more subtle ways and (pale pink) where Rubellite would find the point of greatest need and could be too direct for most. I would prefer using Watermelon Tourmaline for such a powerful healing, but only if the heart centre of clients could handle such a strong energy.

KYANITES

Kyanite is a triclinic crystal that comes in a blue or green colour with silver streaks. It also forms as an orange crystal. There is a grey version as well, although technically this belongs to the Amphibole group of crystals, but on the market, it is known as black or grey Kyanite. Kyanite mainly forms in clusters with blade-like sticks and is also called Disthene, which means double strength. This is because the hardness across the width of a Kyanite blade is 4-5 and along the length it is 6-7.

Blue Kyanite

Blue Kyanite carries a very potent and transformative energy and must not be underestimated. Although it can be placed anywhere in the energy field, it relates strongly to the throat chakra, the shoulder gridline and the causal body. Where Blue Topaz blasts blockages, Blue Kyanite addresses these on more subtle but also more profound levels, especially in cases where substantial change is indicated. The bigger blades are suitable to draw through the auric field and the smaller ones can be used on the gridlines. They can also serve as a bridge between two chakras. Blue Kyanite is particularly suitable for the shoulder line and by placing a small tumbled crystal such as Snowy Quartz behind each blade, the energies are contained towards the energy field. Hematite, Copper, Carnelian and Garnet are some of the suitable grounding crystals for Blue Kyanite.

Green Kyanite

Green Kyanite is not all that easy to find. It is a little less intense than the blue variety, and is one of the green crystals that relates very strongly to nature, especially the Devic energies. This crystal is mainly used in combination with other Kyanites or triclinic crystals, and it can be placed throughout the energy field. Rhodonite combines especially well with Green Kyanite and so does Fossilised Wood, if a gentler energy is needed. Jaspers are also suitable grounders to use with this crystal.

Grey Kyanite

Grey or Black Kyanite is best used for meditation purposes but can bring up fairly dramatic and unpleasant memories, including those of past or 'other' lives (past lives are those we view from a point of an Earthly incarnation, other lives are viewed from a point of awareness which is timeless). Bearing this in mind, Grey Kyanite is therefore not really suitable to use on someone else. This crystal also has a slight Silver sheen and can seem as a little spooky. It can also relate to the more serious energies behind nature which are not necessarily friendly, so when using Grey Kyanite in this way, please be discerning and careful.

Orange Kyanite

Orange Kyanite has an amazing energy that is far more subtle but also more powerful than Carnelian. It is also available in a tumbled version and can then be placed on a chakra. The sacral chakra is the one to which orange Kyanite relates most. It harmonises especially well with other Kyanite crystals, Turquoise, Sunstone and Labradorite.

TOURMALINES

Tourmaline comes in a variety of colours and is pyro-electric (sensitive to heat) as well as piezo-electric (sensitive to pressure). This means that when this crystal is heated or pressured it emits tiny volts of electricity. The energy of Tourmaline is indeed very potent and not suitable for fragile people. One could say that this crystal goes straight to the point of greatest need and it works on all levels, from the spiritual, right down to the etheric. The crystal system of Tourmalines is trigonal and their hardness is 7- 7.5.

The main Tourmalines that are used in healing are:

Rubellite, which is a deep pink to almost red colour
Verdelite, which is a deep green
Indicolite, which is a deep blue colour
Watermelon Tourmaline which is both green and pink
Dravite which is a golden brown
Achroite which is a clear Tourmaline

There are also many other multi-coloured Tourmalines.

All coloured Tourmalines can be used on relevant gridlines, chakras and in patterns, provided the client's energy field is robust. Tourmaline is highly strengthening but can also work its way through stubborn blockages, although in a direct and blasting manner rather than in subtle ways! Tourmaline combines well with most other powerful crystals and Garnet is one of the more appropriate grounding crystals to use with it.

Schorl, a black Tourmaline is rarely used in healing, except for heavy duty-grounding for those who can handle this. It is, however, the most effective crystal to help reduce the negative static from computers or other electrical appliances. It is also the only crystal that seems to thrive on this and, unlike other crystals, only needs to be cleansed from time to time when being used in this manner. Although protective with regard to such negative energies, (because it absorbs and therefore neutralises these to a certain extent), this is not so in relation to one's personal energy field. Black crystals do not deflect energies and rather than keeping negative or unpleasant vibrations at bay, they attract and absorb them.

For personal enhancement and protection with regard to negative energies, crystals such a Lapis Lazuli, Amethyst or Turquoise, to name just a few, are appropriate. If there is a need to deflect any negativity, Silver is also good option. In rare instances, when someone's energy field is full of nasty congestion and debris, one can place a piece of Schorl, for a few moments only, next to one of the lower gridlines or at the bottom of the vertical line, in order to absorb the negative energies, and then carry on with the session.

OTHER CRYSTALS

I have grouped other crystals together according to how well their energies harmonise. This does not mean that they cannot also be used with other crystals. Crystals in each of the groups are placed in alphabetical order.

Group 1

These crystals harmonise well with most other crystals and their energy is not overly intense.

Dumortierite
This crystal looks like Sodalite but has a slightly higher note. It is orthorhombic and can be placed throughout the energy field by way of patterns, on chakras and gridlines. It has both a restful and protective energy. Although it does not have the grounding energy (on mental levels only) of Sodalite, it can help ease tensions in the energy field. It can be placed on any chakra and is one of the deep

blue crystals that relate most to the brow. The hardness of Dumortierite is 7.

Jade

Jade comes in many colours, such as violet, black and white, but the best known is green. Most Jade tumbled stones available are a dark green. This crystal is monoclinic and can be used on the two lower chakras or gridlines. The lighter variety can be placed throughout the energy field. Light green Jade's energy ranges between that of green Aventurine and Prehnite. Its hardness is 6.5.

Prehnite

Prehnite is a pale green and looks much like green Aventurine (without the Mica) but has a slightly faster and higher vibration. Prehnite's energy is smooth and it can be used to ease the energy flow in the field in an enhancing, rather than a calming manner. It combines beautifully with Rose Quartz as well as other Quartz crystals. Prehnite is orthorhombic and also harmonises well with crystals of that specific system. It can be used in most patterns, all gridlines and chakras. Its hardness is 6.5.

A combination of Rose Quartz and Aventurine will emit both a nurturing and stabilizing energy. Grounding this with Fossilized Wood or Green Jasper would complete this theme. Using Prehnite instead of Aventurine would create a far more potent and enhancing rather than stabilizing theme. Grounding these combinations with Garnet would create far more intense energy patterns. The inexperienced eye, however, would barely notice the difference since the crystals look so similar.

Sodalite

Sodalite is a deep blue crystal with occasional white inclusions and harmonises well with most other crystals. It is one of the components of Lapis Lazuli, which is why it could also be placed in group 4. Its crystal system is cubic and it has a stabilising energy which can also help ground energies on mental levels. This is why it is also often used for stress, if this shows up in the relevant layers or chakras in the field. It can be used throughout the energy field and on all of the systems.

Sodalite also has a protective energy that is especially effective because of its 'grounding' element. In this context it is suitable for those for whom the energies of Lapis Lazuli are too intense. The hardness of Sodalite is 5-6. Carnelian, Copper, Pyrite, Jaspers and also Garnets are grounding crystals that harmonise well with Sodalite.

Group 2

The following crystals are suitable for a more fragile energy field. Most of them are amorphous or partly amorphous, and originate either from trees or from the oceans and seas. They can also be combined with many other crystals.

Amber

Amber is fossilized raisin from submerged, extinct coniferous trees and is around three hundred million years old. Most Amber derives from the Baltic Sea and is found in the countries surrounding it. Amber is one of the first substances ever to be used for jewellery thousands of years ago. In the sixteenth and seventeenth centuries it was worth its weight in Gold. The majority of Amber is a bone-white or honey-yellow colour, but it also comes in red, blue, green and purple hues, although this type of Amber is mainly found around the Dominican Republic.

The energy of Amber is like a soft warm glow and it can be used anywhere in the energy field. It is often fashioned into teething rings for babies, which shows how gentle and supportive its energy is. One of the pregnant students on VHF courses reported that the only crystal her unborn baby reacted to was Amber. Amber often contains insect remains although since the release of the movie *Jurassic Park*, which has heightened the popularity of Amber, this is often artificially inserted! In natural Amber the insect remains are rarely intact. Copal, which is a semi fossilized gum, is a substance similar to Amber. Its energy has, however, less substance than that of Amber. It is not as ancient as Amber and around one to two million years old. Copal often contains (natural) fully intact insect remains.

Amber can be used on all chakras, gridlines and on all levels of the energy field. Combining it with other crystals will add to its energy accordingly. Opaque Calcites harmonise well with Amber and so do crystals that are appropriate to address tensions and stresses.

Aragonite

Aragonite is technically the only crystal that is not partly amorphous in this group. It is orthorhombic and comes in a light brown, light grey or white colour. Aragonite can be used anywhere in the energy field and has a gentle and enhancing energy. It relates to Pearl because of the Nacre in it and is therefore placed in this group. It can in certain instances serve as a very gentle grounding crystal.

Coral

Coral is formed by tiny sea creatures and comes in an orange, red or white colour. The orange or red versions are mainly used in healing and on the two lower chakras. It is not very easy to come by and is not often used in healing work. The main difference between Coral and Fire Opal is that Coral has a softer energy. Red Coral would enhance where White Coral would clear.

Jet

Jet is mainly a light grounding crystal. It is black in colour and made of a compressed substance of rotted trees. It is the gentlest black 'crystal' and like all black crystals absorbs energies. It is mostly used with Amber or in combination with flower healing. The only chakra I personally would place it on is the base, for the purpose of absorbing debris, and then I would replace it with another crystal.

Opal

Opal comes in milky white, pink, turquoise, orange, green and black colours. It consists mainly of tiny Silica spheres and water, which is why it should not be placed near a radiator or in strong sunlight. Pink Opal is the one that is most used in healing work. It is much softer than Rose Quartz, but slightly more intense than Mangano Calcite. It combines well with Shell and Pearl, but also with many other crystals when a softer energy is needed.

Pearl

Pearls are also organic and have a soft, flowing energy that is, however, not to be underestimated. One would mainly use Pearl on a chakra to gently open this or clear a small blockage. You could also place it in a pattern with other crystals that have a more flowing type of energy, such as Aquamarine or Opal.

Shell

The main shells that are used in healing are Paua Shell and a Pink Shell, which is slightly softer. Shell is organic and can be used for a fragile energy field because it is so gentle. It combines beautifully with Pearl and also Aragonite. If a slightly stronger energy is needed Aquamarine is also suitable. Shell has a slightly clearing, enhancing as well as inspirational energy.

Shungite

Shungite is mainly formed from Carbon and technically not a crystal. Its main quality is that of clearing on a fairly down-to-earth (etheric) level. For healing or wearing it as a pendant the elite quality is the most appropriate and it seems to help with geopathic stresses. This crystal is mined in Russia. During the Second World War it was used to help purify water when nothing else was available.

Group 3

These crystals all have a somewhat higher and also intense note than the Quartz, Feldspar and Calcite families. They also work well with Spodumenes, Tourmalines, Corundum, Beryls and Garnets.

Apophyllite

Apophyllite is a crystal that can help clear issues on virtually all levels of the energy field. Many healers also have a large piece in their home because of its clearing energy. It is more intense than Snowy Quartz, and therefore more versatile. It comes mainly in a brilliant clear colour but often has inclusions of **Stilbite**, which is a pale salmon coloured crystal. **Stilbite** also forms as clusters by itself. This crystal has a very high note, and can be used on higher levels in the energy field. It relates specifically to the causal layer and can in this context be combined with Celestite, since these two crystals harmonise extremely well.

Green Apophyllite is relatively rare and has a slightly slower energy, which is enhancing rather than clearing. Apophyllite also comes in (translucent) pale grey or pale blue colours and sometimes has tiny red or black inclusions. Drawing it through specific levels of the energy field can help clear debris like no other crystal. The clear variety is not all that often used on energy centres because this would be too intense for most. Apophyllite is tetragonal, has a high water content and most of it is found in India. Apophyllite is a must in a healing kit.

Celestite

Celestite is a translucent pale blue or white crystal. The pale blue variety is found in Madagascar. It has a very fast and potent energy and is often used to help connect with the Angelic, other forms of guidance or the Higher Self. It can also enhance and to a certain extent help clear negativity, but only for those who are comfortable with such a high energy. It therefore needs strong grounders such as Hematite or Garnets. For those who prefer a somewhat lighter grounder, Carnelian is also suitable.

In terms of energy centres, Celestite relates most to the crown or the throat centre, higher layers of the auric field and higher or androgynous grid lines. A less intense version is called **Angellite** which can be used throughout the energy field. This crystal has a slightly stronger energy than both Blue Lace Agate and Blue Calcite. Celestite is orthorhombic and combines well with many other crystals of the same system. Although Prehnite, which is also orthorhombic, is of a lower note than Celestite, it can under certain circumstances be used in combination with it, especially when more than one chakra needs to be addressed or when a pattern of two different type crystals is indicated.

Danburite

Danburite is a translucent, pale pink crystal which also comes in a golden colour similar to that of Golden Beryl. Its vibration is extremely fine and high. It is orthorhombic and, in addition to this group, combines well with crystals such a Tourmalines, Beryls, Kunzite and Hiddenite, Topaz, Ruby and Sapphire. This crystal is mostly used over the crown area and can strengthen one's link to the Angelic or other high energies. It can also be used on the androgynous lines by itself, or with another high vibration crystal on the vertical line.

Danburite is also an excellent crystal for meditation of a high vibration, especially if there is a need to link more strongly to various forms of guidance. At times Light workers can go through a phase that is called the Dark Night of the Soul. In such a case Danburite is one of the most appropriate crystals to use, together with the Bach Flower essence Sweet Chestnut.

Diamond

Diamond is not often used in healing, mainly because of the high cost. Its energy, especially if polished as a gem, would be far too intense for most. Although this crystal is stunning, it does have a quality of greed connected with it, which is another reason it is not all that popular in healing circles. It is interesting to note that Diamond originally derives from the plant kingdom since it starts out as Carbon. It is cubic and is the hardest crystal on the Mohs scale which is 10 and means it can scratch any other crystal. Diamonds come in many colours, such as green, pink, yellow, black, grey, blue and brown. Meditating with Diamond can transport you to other planes of existence.

Fluorite

Fluorite is a beautiful and magical crystal. It comes mostly in green or purple or a combination of both these colours. It also comes in clear, white, pink, black, blue and yellow colours. Fluorite can be used anywhere in the energy field. Its energy is highly inspirational, and it is one of the crystals that is often used to help remember dreams or stimulate creativity. Garnet grounders go especially well with Fluorite since both crystals are cubic. For a gentler energy Wood or Jasper grounders are more appropriate.

Placing someone in a Fluorite pattern can boost the higher mental levels as well as promote creative endeavours. Placed on gridlines it would enhance these and on chakras gently uplift, or alternatively help integrate a higher note. For some this crystal can also be useful in dealing with stress and tensions. Fluorite is a highly versatile crystal since most people can relate with ease to its energy. In meditation it can transport one to places of beauty and inspiration which is something we all need from time to time.

Iolite

Iolite is an orthorhombic crystal with a deep blue colour that can have a hint of violet. This crystal is also called Water Sapphire, because it is similar in appearance to Sapphire. Iolite can also be likened to Sapphire energetically, although it is a little less intense. It relates most to the brow centre but can also be placed over the crown or on the throat if that is appropriate.

Its energy is profound as well as opening and enhancing. Iolite harmonises especially well with other orthorhombic crystals of a high vibration. Like all deep blue crystals, it also has a protective energy. The hardness of Iolite is 7.

Peridot

Peridot is a green crystal that forms in the mantle of the Earth and has as intense a lustre as polished Zircon. It is orthorhombic and can be used anywhere in the energy field. Like many green crystals it relates strongly to nature, or rather the Devic energies that take care of nature, and therefore also has a magical energy. Peridot can be placed on all chakras but relates more to the heart and lower centres. In a pattern it would harmonise beautifully with Danburite, to name just one crystal you can combine it with. Its energy is enhancing in a subtle fashion and it can also be used on gridlines.

Fossilized Wood is a suitable gentle grounder with this crystal and Garnet goes well with it if something more intense is needed. At times Peridot is difficult to distinguish from high grade Grossular Garnet, which can only be used on the lower energy centres and gridlines. Peridot mostly comes in tiny crystals but these can be used in combination with others. Small crystals are highly suitable for distant healing.

Scapolite

Scapolite comes in pale yellow as well as pale purple colours. It is one of the few crystals that are tetragonal, and you can use it anywhere in the energy field. This crystal is striated and much paler than Golden Topaz or most other yellow crystals. It is mainly used for creating a link between other crystals where this is necessary. Its energy is light, although the purple version is slightly stronger.

Vesuvianite

This is another tetragonal crystal which comes in green. It combines well with Scapolite due to the same crystal system, but is not all that much used in healing. It is a little denser than Aventurine, but has a higher note than Garnet. The main reason Scapolite and Vesuvianite have been included in this book is because they are both tetragonal and at times, healers place clients in shapes that mirror the actual crystal system of the crystals they use.

Group 4

This group harmonises extremely well together and has a deep and slightly different note from most of the others which is not easy to describe. The energies are extremely potent in a more solid fashion than those of group 3.

Apatite

Apatite is a rather dense, opaque blue or green crystal which looks slightly mottled. The translucent gem variety, however, is of a much higher and intense vibration and can be used throughout the energy field. Apatite is hexagonal. It therefore combines extremely well with Sugilite and the Beryl family. Darker Apatite is mainly used for grounding, on the base chakra or the lower two gridlines, depending on what other crystals are used.

The gem quality can be suitable to use on the chakra system or gridlines that need a potent and enhancing energy. In this case Apatite also harmonises very well with crystals from group 3. The main colours of gem Apatite are an intense blue and yellowish green. The hardness of Apatite is 5.

Azurite

Azurite is a deep, brilliant blue crystal which sometimes grows together with Malachite. It is also monoclinic and has a hardness of 3.5 to 4. This crystal is mainly suitable for the brow centre for those who can handle such an intense and enriching energy on this chakra. In such a case it would promote one's inner vision in quite a direct and not always comfortable manner.

Azurite, like most deep blue crystals, also has a protective quality. It can be used on gridlines or in patterns, especially if combined with other crystals. Placing it around a person and alternating it with Turquoise would hugely enhance his/her energy field in a protective manner, but only if such a powerful combination is appropriate. To then ground this with either Malachite or Garnet, would be incredibly harmonious, although not suitable for a newcomer to crystalline energies!

Charoite

Charoite is a purple crystal mainly found in Russia. It has a strong energy although somewhat less intense than Sugilite. It has, like all crystals that have a silvery hue, a slightly magical quality. It also has a protective as well as clearing quality, and like all purple crystals strongly relates to the more spiritual qualities. It is monoclinic.

Charoite can be used on all the chakras, gridlines, all levels of the energy field and is appropriate for most patterns. It combines extremely well with Seraphinite. Charoite and Amethyst, placed in an alternating fashion around someone would create a profound spiritual and protective energy pattern. Doing this with Charoite and Snowy Quartz would soften this and change the accent of the theme into that of clearing.

Chrysocolla

Chrysocolla has a high Copper content and its colour is a deep blue green. It often grows together with Malachite and both crystals are monoclinic. Its energy is potent and mainly suitable for the lower chakras and gridlines, although, under certain circumstances it can be placed on the throat chakra. It mainly strengthens and also has a protective quality that can be likened to that of Turquoise, although Chrysocolla is somewhat denser.

Chrysocolla combines beautifully with all the crystals in this group as well as some of the Quartz crystals, especially Carnelian. Meditating with it can help promote creativity, although in a more down to earth manner than Fluorite, which is more inspirational. The hardness of Chrysocolla is 3.5-4.

Copper

Copper is mainly used in healing as a grounding crystal, although one can also place it on the lower two gridlines. The reason it is included in this book is because there are so many crystals with a high Copper content that they combine well with it. Like most metallic crystals Copper is cubic.

Copper also can draw out and absorb unhelpful energies, which is why it is often worn as a bracelet by those that suffer from rheumatic conditions. Copper also is a conductor of energy and can be used in order to link other crystals. The hardness of Copper is 2.5. To clean Copper, put some fresh lemon juice and cider vinegar in a small container, place your Copper piece in it and shake gently for a few moments.

Gold

Gold is very expensive which is one of the reasons it is not used very much in healing. It does, however, have a place in this book and if you can obtain a few small nuggets of Gold for your healing kit, this is definitely worthwhile. Gold absorbs negative energies, so it is always a good idea to clean your jewellery regularly if it contains Gold.

The energies of Gold, are also enhancing and uplifting, in a less intense and more solid fashion than Citrine or Golden Optical Calcite. It combines well with crystals such as Sunstone and Labradorite as well as Garnet to ground the energies. The chakra Gold relates most to is the solar plexus but you could use it on all the others as well. It is also obviously regarded as one of the crystals that relates to abundance. Gold is cubic and has a hardness of 2.5-3.

Lapis Lazuli

Lapis Lazuli, which means blue stone, is made up of six minerals which are Lazulite, Sodalite, Pyrite, Calcite, Hauynite and Noselite. All of these are cubic, except the Calcite which is trigonal. The best quality Lapis is a deep blue with golden Pyrite inclusions, which is mainly mined by hand in Afghanistan. Lapis is one of the crystals that has been known since ancient times, and its energy is strong, profound and also protective.

Lapis can be placed on any of the chakras, although it relates most to the brow. It promotes inner vision and wisdom and is one of the crystals that can help you to access past life experiences. It can also be placed anywhere else in the field, on all gridlines and layers and can be used to form all patterns. Its cubic crystal system could be one of the reasons why Lapis Lazuli can also help to integrate more spiritual qualities within oneself. For those who do not require such a profound energy, Sodalite is more appropriate. Grounding crystals that combine very well with Lapis are Pyrite, Carnelian, Jasper and Garnet. Lapis Lazuli has a hardness of 5.5-6.

Larimar

Larimar is a beautiful turquoise and white coloured crystal. Although similar in colour to Turquoise, it has a much softer and more fluid energy. It can be used anywhere in the energy field, mainly in order to replenish, refresh or slightly uplift. It combines well with most white crystals and work with them to enhance the clearing process.

When Turquoise became more difficult to obtain, I wondered if Larimar could be a worthwhile substitute, especially since its crystal system is also triclinic, but Larimar energy is much lighter and flowing than that of Turquoise and it also does not have a Copper content. The energies of these two crystals are very different. The hardness of Larimar is 4.5-5.

Lepidolite

Lepidolite is a purple crystal with inclusions of Mica which give it a sparkly appearance. Its energy is softer than all the other purple crystals and it can be placed anywhere in the energy field. Lepidolite is monoclinic. Big Lepidolite crystals are stunning and excellent to meditate with. They can help transport one to the more pleasant parts of the astral world and also to the higher mental levels if in need of inspiration. Even Spiritual levels can be reached with relative ease with this crystal in a subtle and gentle manner.

With regard to healing work, one could place someone in a pattern of Charoite and Lepidolite if two different types of strength were indicated. One could then ground this with Yellow Jasper or Pyrite in order to complement the colours, Hematite in order to complement the silver sparks in these crystals or Garnet to intensify it all. The possibilities of this crystal are endless! Lepidolite is monoclinic and its hardness is 2.5-3.

Malachite

Beautiful and vibrant, the energy of Malachite is a little deceptive. Because of its green colour many may think it suitable for the heart centre, but Malachite is quite dense and only appropriate for the lower energy centres and gridlines. It is also suitable for grounding. Malachite has a high Copper content and can help draw out negative energies that then need to be cleared. It is a powerful and earthly crystal that is also often used by Shamanic healers.

For someone with a fairly robust energy field, whose brow and base chakras required potent energies, one could use Malachite on the base and Azurite on the brow and then ground this with Copper. In order to balance out this scenario, Turquoise on either the sacral, solar plexus or throat could then also be suitable. Harmony is always important! Malachite is often fashioned in ornaments; its crystal system is monoclinic and the hardness 4.

Pyrite

Pyrite, also called Fool's Gold is mainly used for grounding purposes. It is one of the components of Lapis Lazuli and therefore harmonises well with that crystal. If you put Red Garnet together with Pyrite you feel you can manifest virtually anything. With regard to colour, purple and gold are complementary so it can be used as a grounder for crystals such as Sugilite. Pyrite is cubic and actually forms in cubes. Its hardness is 6-6.5.

Chalcopyrite is a crystal which is both black and gold and sometimes confused with Pyrite. Its hardness is 3.5-4 and its crystal system is tetragonal. This crystal is only suitable for grounding, although you can also use it for profound meditation relating to more earthly issues.

Rhodochrosite

Rhodochrosite comes in a pale to vibrant pink colour and its crystal system is trigonal. The palest version can be used throughout the energy field although it is not all that suitable for the higher energy centres. If one compares it with other pink crystals it ranges somewhere between Strawberry Quartz without black inclusions and Rhodonite. Its energy mainly strengthens and enhances.

Rhodochrosite is trigonal and its hardness is 4. The gem quality of this crystal is more intense and mainly suitable for the sacral and base chakras and lower gridlines. Unpolished Rhodochrosite is more versatile because its energy is then much softer.

Seraphinite

Seraphinite, also called Clinochlore is a green and white crystal with a silvery glow. Like Charoite it is mainly found in Russia and combines well with this crystal although it has a slower energy. It is monoclinic and can be used on the lower chakras and gridlines, especially if combined with Charoite and Silver. Hematite or Garnet are excellent grounders to use with Seraphinite.

Seraphinite is also one of the crystals that can connect one strongly to the energies behind nature. Where Charoite links more with the Angelic itself, Seraphinite connects to Devic energies, especially those of the plant kingdom. It therefore also harmonises well with crystals such as Amber and Fossilised Wood. The hardness of Seraphinite is 2-2.5

Silver

Silver is not a metal that is often used in healing but it definitely has a place. Small polished Silver pieces combine beautifully with crystals such as Blue, Green and Grey

Kyanite, Sunstone, Lepidolite, Charoite, Seraphinite and any other crystal that has a silver spark. It is then best used in a pattern or on gridlines, together with one of these crystals.

Silver also deflects energies and could be used in this way to create a boundary with regard to negative energies. In this case a small piece could even be placed briefly on an affected chakra. Silver relates to the Moon, and therefore also all that is intuitive, feminine and so forth. Small unpolished pieces of Silver are quite dark and could serve as grounding crystals. Silver is Cubic and has a hardness of 2.5-3. It does not really belong in this group, but I have placed it here because a number of other metals are included.

Sugilite

Sugilite is a crystal mainly found in South Africa. It was discovered in the1970s', around the same time as the planet Chiron. It mainly comes in a deep purple and it is hexagonal, which is why it combines well with the Beryl family and Apatite. Sugilite has an intense and powerful energy and works on many levels, including the etheric. For those who are interested in the seven ray teachings, Amethyst is the crystal that traditionally relates to the seventh ray of order, manifestation and magic.

I personally, however, find the energies of Sugilite far more appropriate in this regard, since they are more solid. Sugilite can be used throughout the energy field and on all the systems where such a powerful energy is appropriate.

Strengthening, unblocking in an intense manner and protective to a certain extent are its main qualities. It is not easy to obtain any longer and the energy that comes closest to it with regard to purple crystals is Charoite, although this is not as potent.

Turquoise

Turquoise has for centuries been used as a healing crystal and is unfortunately becoming quite rare. It has a strong energy and is traditionally known as a protective and strengthening crystal. It also associates with ancestral patterns. It can be used anywhere in the energy field, but relates strongly to the throat, solar plexus and sacral chakras. Its crystal system is triclinic which could be a reason that it can also be helpful with issues of change, when our energy field can be a little weaker than usual.

If someone's energy field needs strengthening and if they can handle a potent energy, an oval of Lapis Lazuli crystals alternating with Turquoise would be highly effective. The most harmonious grounders when using Turquoise are Copper, Carnelian, at times Malachite and also Obsidian. It just depends on the individual one is working with! The hardness of Turquoise is 5-6.

Group 5

This little group mainly has a clearing energy of quite a profound nature and both Realgar and Sulphur are very toxic so please use with care.

Halite

Halite is a Salt and must therefore not be placed in water, since it would dissolve. It is an excellent crystal to help clear debris from the auric field or, when appropriate, from a chakra, gridlines or the auric field. The energy of Halite is strong and a little more penetrating than the energy of Snowy Quartz. Salt, especially Himalayan Salt is often fashioned into lamps which when lit emit a beneficial energy to help keep the air clean. It is also sometimes fashioned into small spheres. Halite is cubic and has a hardness of 2.

Realgar

Realgar is an orange to red crystal and beautiful to look at. It contains Arsenic and is not often used in healing. It can, however, in rare cases, help draw out highly toxic and poisonous energies. In such a scenario, one would place a small piece of it underneath the base of the spine for a brief moment, and then continue with other methods to help clear the client's energy field. It is important to wash one's hands after touching it. Realgar is monoclinic and its hardness is 1.5.

Sulphur

Sulphur is an excellent crystal to draw out impurities. It is mainly used on the three lower chakras but relates most to the solar plexus. It is less dense than Malachite which also draws out negativity and therefore a little more appropriate for those who cannot handle heavy energies.

When using Sulphur in this way, you should replace it with another crystal once the negative energies have been absorbed. Sulphur is monoclinic and its hardness is 1.5 to 2.

Group 6

These crystals are mainly grounders, except Zircon which does not really fit with any of the other groups.

Chiastolite

Chiastolite, also called the cross stone, is a medium grounder. It is slightly heavier than Petrified Wood but each piece has a distinctive cross formation, which makes the energies more precise. This crystal works well as a grounder when specific geometric patterns are used. It is orthorhombic and its hardness is 7.5.

Hematite

Hematite is an Iron ore. It looks like a metallic silver crystal but if you cut a piece of it in half you can see the red ore. This crystal is a heavy-duty grounder and only suitable for those who can handle such a strong energy. It works well with high energy crystals such as Kyanite or Celestite when a deeper grounding is required. **Galena** looks similar but is even denser and not used very often in healing work. Hematite is trigonal and has a hardness of 6.5.

Rhodonite

Rhodonite is a deep pink crystal with black inclusions. The gem quality is a deep red. This crystal is a medium grounder and works beautifully with Rose Quartz. It can be used on the base chakra and two lower gridlines. To ground the quality of harmony, one could place the client in a pattern of Rose Quartz or crystals of a similar frequency and then ground this pattern with Rhodonite. Rhodonite is triclinic and combines especially well with Amazonite and green or grey Kyanite. Its hardness is 5.5-6.5.

Zircon

Zircon is one of the oldest crystals on the planet and, when polished, has a stronger lustre than Diamond. It used to be called the poor person's Diamond for that reason, especially since it is not expensive. Unpolished Zircon looks like a brown rusty crystal, but the polished version is spectacular and is often fashioned into jewellery. The brown version is mainly used as a grounder. Zircon is tetragonal and has a hardness of 7.5.

Glasses

Moldavite

Moldavite is a stunning green glass that was formed when a meteor landed on Earth in Romania. It is amorphous and does indeed have what can be described as a 'cosmic' energy. It has a high note and is excellent for profound meditation.

Like Obsidian, there is more to Moldavite than meets the eye, and for some its energy can be a little too intense in the way that it creates a feeling of being 'spaced out'. It is not a crystal that is often used in healing, but when it is, it is mainly suitable for use on the crown centre. It can then be used in combination with other crystals that are of a faster vibration.

Obsidian

Obsidian is a volcanic glass and, in ancient times, was fashioned into weapons such as knives, arrow heads and spears. Many also use Obsidian spheres or mirrors for scrying, and the best-known historical figure that did this was Nostradamus, who used his Obsidian mirror (in addition to Astrology) to glimpse the future. In healing, this stone is mainly used for grounding, although the black variety can have the opposite effect for some.

Meditating with Black Obsidian can bring deep fears to the fore, which is OK, provided you wish to address these! Mahogany Obsidian is a brown variety with black inclusions and Snowflake Obsidian is black with white (Feldspar) inclusions. Both of these are mainly used for grounding purposes. Apache Tears are a variety of Obsidian that is found in riverbeds in the USA. When polished these are translucent and look a little like dark Smokey Quartz.

Stones

Stones are the most fundamental part of the mineral kingdom but no less important than others. They have their own energy and although not often used in healing, they deserve to be mentioned. I remember when I was once on a holiday on a Greek island, walking on a beautiful beach, I saw seven small white and seven small black stones close to the edge of the sea. I picked them up and had the feeling it was a gift from the elements. Back home in the UK, I experimented with them and found that their energy was helping to clear parts of my energy field in a very gentle and 'down to Earth' manner. The black stones absorbed the unhelpful energies and the white ones cleared whatever had not been absorbed. I still have these little stones.

On one of the first healing courses I facilitated in Ireland, I told the group that they were welcome to bring their personal stones (meaning their crystals). I was somewhat surprised that the next day there was a huge array of actual stones in the room. I took this as a message from the mineral kingdom, and we finished that day with an Earth healing during which the energies became quite potent. During that course I also had the opportunity to experiment on a colleague, and found that stones can be used in combination with crystals with a medium energy, in order to create a more overall solidness. Although they are too dense to place on energy centres or over the crown, they can be placed elsewhere in the field on certain occasions.

I have a big Granite pebble in my car which helps me to stay grounded and a number of stones from various countries that are sometimes used in Earth healing mandalas. I know several people who have bowls of ordinary but pretty stones on their coffee table, and they do emit a basic but lovely energy. On the last course I facilitated in Ireland, one of the participants gave us a bag of beautiful tumbled stones, which she had tumbled herself! Stones, more often than not, have tiny inclusions of Quartz, so they can also be tuned for various purposes.

If you are interested in stone energies, it is worthwhile to go to a stone circle and get a sense of the overall energies. Stonehenge is usually full of people, but another imposing stone circle in Avesbury is often a little quieter and well worth the trip. If you find yourself in a mountainous landscape, take a rest and link specifically to the rocks and stones. You could find this surprisingly powerful, and it is something I would advise any healer to try out. If you have developed your inner hearing, you may well hear a deep sound, which can only be described as awesome and majestic.

Appendix I

GROUNDING CRYSTALS

This is a list of grounding crystals for easy reference. You may find that at different times you require different crystals to help you to ground. The way to choose a grounding crystal for yourself is to establish first what it feels like to be grounded. Then, whilst linked to the Light, pick up a few grounding crystals and select the most effective one. If this feels unpleasant, opt for one with a slightly less intense grounding energy. I have divided the grounding crystals into potent, medium and gentle.

Potent Grounding Crystals
Black Tourmaline
Chiastolite
Galena
Red, Green and Black Garnet
Hematite
Obsidian (can unground for some individuals)
Ruby
Tiger Iron

Medium Grounding Crystals
Apatite (dark green)
Botswana Agate
Bixbite & Black Beryl
Carnelian

Copper
Jade (dark green or black)
Jaspers
Malachite
Petrified Wood
Pyrite
Rhodonite
Smokey Quartz
Tiger's Eye
Zircon (dark brown)

Gentle Grounding Crystals
Amber
Aragonite
Red and Orange Calcite
Coral
Desert Rose
Jet
Septarian
Stones (ordinary)
Unakite

Appendix II

MOHS HARDNESS SCALE

In order to take good care of your crystals it is important to know their hardness. Crystals that are higher on the scale can scratch those that are lower, so it is best not to place or transport these in the same container. All **Quartz** crystals mentioned have a hardness of 7. The exception is **Herkimer Diamond** which has a hardness of 7.5. All **Beryls** have a hardness of 8. Please note that in a number of gemmology books the Mohs hardness scale varies slightly. Next to the hardness number you will find the crystal system of each of the stones for easy reference.

Amber 2.5 Amorphous
Alabaster 2 Monoclinic
Aragonite 3.5-4 Orthorhombic
Apatite 5 Hexagonal
Apophyllite 4 Tetragonal
Azurite 3.5-4 Monoclinic
Calcite 3 Trigonal
Celestite 3-3.5 Orthorhombic
Charoite 5-6 Monoclinic
Chiastolite 7.5 Orthorhombic
Chrysocolla 3.5-4 Monoclinic
Chrysoprase 6-7 Trigonal
Copper 2.5 Cubic
Coral 3-4 Amorphous, Trigonal

Danburite 7 Orthorhombic
Desert Rose 2 Monoclinic
Diamond 10 Cubic
Dumortierite 7 Orthorhombic
Fluorite 4 Cubic
Galena 2.5 Cubic
Garnet 6.5-7.5 Cubic
Gold 2.5-3 Cubic
Halite 2 Cubic
Hematite 5-6 Trigonal
Hiddenite 6.5-7.5 Monoclinic
Iolite 7- 7.5 Orthorhombic
Jade 6-7 Monoclinic
Jet 2 Amorphous
Kunzite 6.5-7.5 Monoclinic
Kyanite across4-5 Triclinic
Kyanite along 6-7 Triclinic
Labradorite 6.5 Triclinic
Lepidolite 2.5-3 Monoclinic
Larimar 5 Triclinic
Lapis Lazuli 5.5-6 Cubic
Malachite 3.5-4 Monoclinic
Moldavite 5 Amorphous
Moonstone 6-6.5 Monoclinic
Obsidian6 Amorphous
Oligoclase 5.5-6 Triclinic
Opal 5.5-6.5 Amorphous
Pearl 2-2.5 Amorphous, Orthorhombic
Peridot 6.5-7 Orthorhombic

Prehnite	6	Orthorhombic
Pyrite	6-6.5	Cubic
Realgar	1.5-2	Monoclinic
Rhodochrosite	4	Trigonal
Rhodonite	6	Triclinic
Ruby	9	Trigonal
Rutile	6-6.5	Tetragonal
Sapphire	9	Trigonal
Satin Spar	2	Monoclinic
Scapolite	5-6	Tetragonal
Selenite	2	Monoclinic
Septarian	3	Trigonal
Seraphinite	5-6	Monoclinic
Shell	2.5	Amorphous
Shungite	3.5-4	Amorphous
Silver	2.5	Cubic
Sodalite	5-6	Cubic
Sugilite	6	Hexagonal
Sulphur	1.5-2	Orthorhombic
Sunstone	6	Triclinic
Topaz	8	Orthorhombic
Tourmaline	7.5	Trigonal
Turquoise	5	Triclinic
Unakite	6	Monoclinic
Vesuvianite	6.5	Tetragonal
Zircon	7.5	Tetragonal

Appendix III

List of most Meditations and Self-Healing Exercises

Chapter 17

Chapter 28

A Few Recommended Books

Below are a few books that those who study any form of healing may find helpful. They are a slightly dated, because I have not read much these past years and can therefore not include more current books. The reason only few books on crystals are included is that most I have read, although containing valid information, mention that specific crystals are appropriate for certain physical symptoms and conditions which is not my experience.

Healing:

- Vibratonal Medicine by Richard Gerber
- Wheels of Life by Anodea Judith
- Anatomy of the Spirit by Caroline Myss (and her other books)
- The Healing Power of Illness by Dethlefsen & Dahlke
- Hands of Light by Barbara.Ann Brennan
- Cutting the Ties that Bind by Phyllis Krystal

Inner Development:

- Advanced Course in Yogi Philosophy) by Yogi Ramacharaka (and his other books)
- The Shack by Wm Paul Young
- The Power of Now by Eckart Tolle (and his other books)
- All the books written by Dr Wayne W. Dyer are highly inspirational and most relate to manifesting your life

Crystals 'scientific':

- Rocks & Minerals of the World An Illustrated Encyclopedia
- Crystals by Ian Mercer (a Natural History Museum Publication)
- Field Guide to the Rocks & Minerals of the World by Larousse

Crystal Healing:

- Gem elixirs and Vibrational Healing by Gurudas
- Crystals & Healing for Everyone by Henriette Maasdijk (a book for beginners)
- Crystal Power, Crystal Healing by Michael Gienger

Colour and Sound:

- Form, Sound and Colour Healing by Theo Gimbel
- Healing with Sound by Olivia Dewhurst Maddock
- Nada Brama The World is Sound by Joachim E. Berendt

Flower Essences:

- Bach Flower Remedies by P.M. Chancellor
- The Healing Herbs of Edward Bach by Julian and Martine Barnard (and their other books)
- Bach Flower Therapy by Mechtild Scheffer

Miscellaneous:

- The Power of Your Subconscious Mind by Dr Joseph Murphy
- A handbook of Angels by HC Moolenburgh
- Messages from Water by Masaru Emoto
- Psychic Protection by William Bloom
- You are Energy by Henriette Maasdijk

Glossary

Affirmation *a short, positive sentence that you repeat frequently in order to help create something.*

Akashic Records *a place in the worlds of energy where everything that has happened, is happening and will happen is contained.*

Angel *Beings of Light created by the Universal Consciousness (God). They maintain order and beauty in the cosmos, are in charge of nature and often help human beings in many different ways. The name Angel means messenger.*

Astral *the astral world is the one closest to the physical world.*

Atlantis *a legendary civilization that preceded ours. It was destroyed by earthquakes and sank into (what many believe) is the Atlantic Ocean. This happened as a consequence of the misuse of power (including that of crystals) by the elite.*

Auric Field *the electromagnetic field that surrounds every living organism, including that of human beings. It is also called the bio-magnetic field, energy field, aura or just the field.*

Clairaudient *'clear hearing' and relates to those who can hear sounds that are not audible to others*

Clairvoyant *'clear seeing' and relates to those who can perceive images others cannot, including sometimes events o happening in the future.*

Curse *a strong expression of hate projected towards an individual or a family, often with the aid of invoked supernatural dark forces. There exist also cursed objects such as jewels, figurines or furniture.*

Elemental *a nature spirit relating to one of the elements (water, earth, fire or air).*

Devic *the Devic kingdom is a term for all the nature spirits in existence.*

Druid *Druids were philosophers, sages, priests, herbalists and teachers and were considered a high-ranking class before the emergence of Christianity. They worshipped nature and were highly accomplished in magical practices. Their origin was Celtic. Modern day Druidism is a recognized religion and its followers promote harmony and reverence for the natural world.*

Entity *the meaning of entity in this book is an unpleasant or malicious energy.*

Geode *geodes are hollow rock formations lined with crystals. Amethyst geodes, often called Madonnas, are one example.*

Glamour *in these pages' glamour relates to delusion and fantasy that is often experienced by those who start out in learning about the worlds of energy.*

Gnome *an elemental relating to earth*

Guru *a revered teacher who has many followers who, without question, take on board all his/her teachings.*

Healing crisis *when symptoms or issues intensify during or after a healing session.*

Higher Self *one of the higher aspects of a human being*

Karma *the law of cause and effect. What goes around comes around is a popular saying with regard to karma.*

Kundalini *a life-force located at the base of the spine and related to a divine feminine goddess according to Hindu mythology*

Light *in this book Light with a capital L relates to Universal Consciousness as well as high vibrational energies that are channeled by healers.*

Magic *the application of invoked natural and other-worldly forces in order to achieve something.*

Mandala *a circular pattern that can be made with crystals, pebbles flowers or sand. They can help to bring subconscious issues to the fore, especially when you randomly draw patterns (or anything else) into a circle on a blank piece of paper.*

Mantra *specific repetitive phrases that have been thought, voiced and chanted over thousands of years.*

Medium *someone who can communicate with spirits (of the departed).*

Mohs hardness *measures the hardness of minerals in relation to harder minerals scratching softer ones.*

Mystery school *a school that teaches ancient (eternal) wisdom.*

Mystic *A person who wants to raise their vibration to levels that they can join the Light*

New Age *a term for everything pertaining to healing, inner development and related practices that started in the 1960ties.*

Occultist *a person who wants to bring the highest possible vibration of Light they can embody down to Earth*

Pagan *a pre-Christian religion that worships where more than one God is worshipped. All Pagan religions have a great reverence for the natural world.*

Psychic *someone who has a highly developed sixth sense.*

Psychic Attack *causing harm by the projection of negativity onto someone.*

Psychometry *the ability to obtain in-depth information about the history of an object and its owners by holding it.*

Salamander *an elemental relating to fire.*

Seeker s*omeone who never stops delving deeper into a subject.*

Shaman *A healer who works to great extent with the animal and/or plant kingdoms. Some Shamans are also strongly connected to their ancestors in the spirit world and versed in astral travel. Shamans from different cultures have slightly different traditions.*

Signature *an impression that helps to identify a specific energetic experience or a specific other-worldly being.*

Soul *the highest aspect of a human being.*

Spirit *an 'other-worldly' being.*

Subtle bodies *various levels of the human energy field.*

Subtle planes *different levels in the worlds of energy.*

Subtle anatomy *the human subtle energy systems.*

Subtle physiology *the function of the human subtle energy systems.*

Sushumna *one of three subtle energy pathways, which are intertwined along the spine, starting at the base and ending at the* *top in the medulla oblongata. Sushumna is the centre pathway and Ida and Pingala are the other two which are situated on either side, winding upwards.*

Sylph *an elemental relating to air.*

Symbol *a mark or sign that represents something specific.*

Talisman *a symbol or inscription on an object that has magical powers.*

Tarot *A deck of cards used for personal insights or to predict the future.*

Ting Sha *two small cymbals on either side of a string that, when struck, emit a high pitched sound.*

Tibetan Bowl *Bowls constructed of six different metals that, when struck, emit beautiful sounds.*

Trance *the practice of healing or mediumship through being taken over by a non-incarnate being.*

Undine *and elemental relating to water.*

Visualization *in this book it means to imagine something.*

Wiccan *Wicca is a Pagan religion. Most followers are highly experienced herbalists and they are also accomplished in magical practices.*

About the Author

Henriette Maasdijk is of Dutch origin and has lived in London for close to forty years. She is the principal and founder of the Vibrational Healing Foundation, a school for healing and inner development, which was established in 1996. Henriette has taught in Europe, Ireland and the UK, leading diploma courses in subtle energy medicine and related subjects. She was the initiator of the project 'Light in Ireland', which consisted of advanced Light work, facilitated during three weekends, over a period of 10 years in that beautiful country. She now mainly focusses on courses for healers who want to take their work to further levels and those who want to go deeply into the subject of inner development.

Henriette has always had a keen interest in the so-called unknown and a great love and respect for the beauty and power of crystals and also that of nature itself. She believes that self-awareness and healing are the key to a life of joy, empowerment and fulfilment. She also believes that Light work is a crucial factor in helping to create a world with more harmony in it.

About the Vibrational Healing Foundation

The VHF, formed in 1996, offers expert training in the fields of healing, crystal healing and inner development. In the ancient wisdom schools, the dictum 'man know thyself' conveyed best what such training represents; nowadays, it comes under the term 'subtle energy medicine'.

Subtle energy medicine, in a nutshell, is about the exploration of ourselves as complex beings of energy, existing in a world of energy, and how this relates to our life, health and wellbeing. It is also about being able to support others, when they need it, with the skilled use of tools such as crystals, flowers, flower essences, colour and sound. Such work and study are an ongoing process, because this is also a path towards what is termed enlightenment.

For information on courses and workshops please visit:
vibrationalhealingfoundation.co.uk

About the Federation of Subtle Energy Medicine

The VHF is a member of the Federation of Subtle Energy Medicine (FSEM) which is an umbrella organisation whose purpose is to set and uphold high professional standards of training and practice in the healing arts and inner development. Members work in close co-operation, harmony and goodwill, maintaining individual styles and expertise whilst adhering to FSEM standards. All practitioners on the register are highly experienced and adhere to a strict code of conduct.

For information about regulations and to finds a subtle energy medicine therapist or training school in the UK, please visit:
subtlehealth.org

Printed in Great Britain
by Amazon

44624551R00208